Cookin' H
With
One Foot Out The Door

From The Bad Girls Of Natural Foods

Polly Pitchford & Delia Quigley

The Book Publishing Company
Summertown, Tennessee

© 1994 Polly Pitchford & Delia Quigley
All rights reserved. Published in the United States by
The Book Publishing Company, P.O. Box 99
Summertown, TN 38483

Cover by Nava Atlas
Interior design by Barbara McNew
Cover Photos by Evelyn England, Va-Voom Productions

Library of Congress Cataloging-in-Publication Data
Pitchford, Polly, 1956-
   Cookin' healthy with one foot out the door : quick meals for
fast times / Polly Pitchford and Delia Quigley..
   p. cm.
   Includes index.
   ISBN 0-913990-86-8
   1. Vegetarian cookery.   2. Quick and easy cookery.
3. Vegetarianism. I. Quigley, Delia. II. Title
TX837.P567 1994
641.5'636—dc20   93-43471
                                       CIP

ISBN 0-913990-86-8

0 9 8 7 6 5 4 3 2

Calculations for the nutritional analyses in this book are based on the average number of servings listed with the recipes and the average amount of an ingredient if a range is called for. Calculations are rounded up to the nearest gram. If two options for an ingredient are listed, the first one is used. Not included are fat used for frying, unless the amount is specified in the recipe, optional ingredients, or servings suggestions.

CONTENTS

 Indicates recipes that take 15 minutes or less to *prepare and cook!*

To Err Is Human
To Forgive Divine

This is for all you humans who tend to "err" more often than not. We suggest that you forgive yourself for deeds best left unspoken when it comes to discussions of personal diet. Who hasn't gone back for thirds and fourths despite the tightening girth? What fool decided that ice cream should only be served in ½ cup quantities or that once the chip bag is open you're only going to eat that 1 oz.?

Frozen food companies are making a killing from quick meals that take no time in the microwave, but what is it that you're eating? Can the QUALITY of this food nutritionally support your physical, mental, and spiritual well-being? We are so sure that you do not lay awake at night pondering these questions, we decided to write this book to insure that you get a more nutritionally balanced diet without giving up too much of your time to cooking.

O.K., so the microwave takes 10 minutes from the fridge to the table, big deal! What's your hurry? Here is one of the most important and enjoyable events of the day, and you're going to rush it. Sheesh! This is the time to nurture yourself, your family, your dog, your cat, whatever. You like to eat, right? So try taking a little more time, chew your food slowly, enjoy the flavors and textures of your food, get down, and have some fun.

O.K., so for the one hundredth time, you're going to give it a try. Your doctor, kids, wife, husband, parents have all told you that your health is looking pretty shaky and that you need to lose anywhere from 20-150 pounds. Maybe you caught a good glimpse of yourself as you passed the hall mirror and wondered who let the fat person in. When you finally realized that you were looking at your own reflection, you vowed to change your unhealthy ways once and for all. You're not alone. Millions of people are attempting to change their lives through diet and exercise. The question is how do I start? (Make a decision.) How much time will it take? (How long does it take to boil water?) Do I have to give up my favorite animals—beef and chicken? (If you're eating them, yes.) Will I end up joining some religious cult and live on soy burgers for the rest of my life? (That's up to you.) Will I grow my hair long and flash the peace sign at total strangers? (Anything's possible.) Or most frightening, will I buy a pair of those strange looking Birkenstock sandals? (No comment.)

Mind you, these are all valid and crucial questions when one contemplates changing very serious aspects of one's life. Like food, for instance. "You are what you eat" is not to be scoffed at. Food can provide you with the proper nutrition to feed and nourish every cell in your body. As a result, you have plenty of energy, beautiful skin and hair, vibrant eyes, and maybe even a sparkling personality.

"Oh, Delia, you're embarrassing me."

"Easy, Polly, I wasn't talking about your sparkling personality, I was talking about mine."

The other side of the coin is a refined, high-fat, excess animal protein diet, (now you're on familiar territory) which can back up the whole digestive system, dump toxins into the blood stream, and cost you large amounts of money for doctors, hairdressers, dentists, and cosmetic surgery.

As you begin to eat more unrefined vegetarian foods and fewer animal-based meals, you will begin to notice certain changes. You'll probably have more energy, the quality of your skin will improve, you'll be satisfied eating less food (you'll have to trust us on this one), drop a few pounds, and no longer be constipated. (See Q & A on page 9)

Yes, it's true. All this and more can be yours without a great deal of effort, time, or mental gymnastics. Where do I sign up? Read on..........................

?
What Is Healthy Fast Food
?

There is no such animal in this day and time, if we're talking about high-fat hamburgers and french fries. Don't let them try to tell you otherwise, oh seeker of health. However, the healthy fast foods, we write about in this handy little health manual (disguised as a cookbook) are complete vegetarian meals which take under one hour to prepare and cook.

The majority of foods can be purchased from your favorite grocery store with some specialty items found in either the health food store (oh gawd, that hippie place) or oriental food stores. Certain canned, frozen, jarred, boxed, bagged, and aseptic items (try to say that fast five times), will be used along with fresh vegetables and whole grains to make these NUTRITIOUS, BALANCED, DELICIOUS MEALS.

We have provided a list of products with each recipe that have passed the *D&P Healthy Eats Seal of Approval*. Mind you, not an easy test to pass.

As we, Polly and Delia, refugees from the health food store, made our way down the local grocery store aisle, we became overwhelmed and slightly faint by the numerous low-grade options available to the food consumer. To our dismay, we found that the majority of goods were laden with refined sugars, preservatives, artificial flavorings and colorings, conditioners, sodium, chemicals, and lard. (Now, try saying that fast five times).

Stunned by our discovery, we wondered aloud if we were in a scientific grocery lab. Whatever happened to the humble food market? Nonetheless, with much persistence and careful food label inspections, we were pleasantly surprised to find enough items that would pass our D&P H.E.S.O.P. (see previous page) to fill your pantry shelves with the potential for some quick but delicious meals.

Believe it or not, there can be vast differences in opinion as to what people think is fast when preparing food. There are those of the hard core variety who want only to open a can, a bag, and the refrigerator in order to complete the evening's meal. Baking may be a bit much, unless we're talking frozen dinner in the microwave, which you and any two-year-old already know how to do.

Just know that whatever the recipes in this book call for, they can be done by your own rules and need for speed. If we say fresh, you can use frozen, no problem. (If we say tomato, you say tomahto, we say potato, you say potahto). When you're about to go out of your mind reading the number of times we ask you to mince garlic and chop onion, just pull the garlic jar out of the fridge and the bag of frozen pre-chopped onions out of the freezer, and proceed. Suit yourself.

The same goes for the sugar issue. Use it. Refined or not. Brush your teeth with it, use it as a facial scrub, whatever. Just promise us you'll try some of the other sweeteners we use in our recipes. Giving up sugar is not the end of your life, just the beginning of a whole new adventure.

?
What Is
A Vegetarian
And Why
?

Vegetarians are skinny, pale, pimply, humorless, and generally poor dressers, right? Some famous vegetarians include Madonna, Paul and Linda McCartney, Delia Quigley, Polly Pitchford, and Sting. So you see, you're going to have to start changing your ideas about us.

Reasons for being a vegetarian include:

A. Can't stand the sight of blood.

B. Hate getting fur caught between your teeth.

C. Love the taste of plain tofu.

D. Don't want to die from (pick one):

    1. Cancer

    2. Heart disease

    3. Obesity

    4. High blood pressure

    5. Stroke

    6. Fish bone caught in the throat

Vegetarian HOTLINE

With Delia And Polly

Dear Delia and Polly,

I am 12 years old and I want to become a vegetarian just like you. My mom says I won't be able to get enough protein unless I eat meat, but that would be like eating my cat Miffy. I am torn. What do you advise?

Torn

Dear Torn,

Go ahead and eat Miffy. No, just kidding. Do you remember the expression that says mothers know best? Well, in this case it's wrong. You can get plenty of protein from eating a well-rounded vegetarian diet. There are varying amounts of protein in all foods. So be a good girl, and eat your vegetables, grains, beans, nuts, and seeds. You'll grow up to be big and strong like your cat Miffy. Plus, those old boogie men cholesterol and saturated fat won't be found hiding under your bed.

Dear Delia And Polly,

Please excuse the Milky Way chocolate stain on the paper, but I am desperate to break my sugar habit. Help! I'm addicted. How do I stop, because my hips won't stop—growing, that is!

Hershey Kisses

Hershey Kisses

Dear Kisses,

Please excuse the coconut carob fudge stains in this letter. We can certainly relate, because we've been there, dear little Hershey. Try the sugar-free dessert recipes in this book, for breakfast, lunch, and dinner, if you must. Your body will gradually adjust to using lesser amounts of higher quality sweeteners. Begin to eat less candy and cake, and instead eat more whole grains and sweet vegetables, such as carrots, onions, sweet potatoes, and winter squash. Soon your hips won't be craving those Ho-Ho's and Little Debbie cakes, and you will be feeling more balanced and in control of your diet.

Dear Delia and Polly,

Nothing's worked so far! I've had all the tests, the Mayo Clinic couldn't help me, and the best doctors in the country are baffled! Please, you're my last hope! I have ... fat ankles and my hands swell; but worst of all, I am always thirsty. I drink at least eight glasses of water a day and just swell some more. (I particularly notice this right after I finish eating a bag of corn chips.) What could all this mean? Can you solve my dilemma???

Salty Tears

Dear S.T.,

Duhhh!!!!! Gee, Pol, what do you think? Gosh, I don't know, Delia, sounds like it could be the NaCl blues to me. Salt, that is, sodium chloride, corn chips, hot dogs, hard cheese, processed meat, diet cola. (This must be sung to the tune of the Beverly Hillbillies theme song, for full effect.) Dry those salty tears and get your hand out of the chip bag, girl. You've asked the right question at the right time to the right people. The magic words here are: moderation, lo-salt, herbs, and unprocessed foods. You'll notice as you peruse our recipes that you can choose between sea salt (which retains its minerals), Bragg Amino Acid (La mystery liquid made from soybeans), soy sauce (a little dab will do ya), and just herbs to enhance the flavor. Buy unsalted packaged and canned items whenever possible, and don't put the salt shaker on the table. Good luck and happy saline!

Dear Delia and Polly,

I want to look like Raquel, but I hear she never eats cheese, milk, or butter, and yet her bazoombas look better than ever! Is there life after dairy, and how is it possible?

Elsie

Dear Elsie,

First of all you'll notice in our photo that our dairy-free bazoombas can hold their own, and you'll also notice that in our recipes we use soy cheese as a perfect replacement for dairy cheese. If it's calcium you're worried about, then don't, because you can find plenty of it in dark leafy greens, nuts, seeds, broccoli, dried fruit, and beans. This way you can avoid the high fat/cholesterol boogie person, and your body is better able to absorb this mineral. So forget the liposuction and implants and go dairy-free. Your cellulite will hate you!

Dear Delia and Polly,

What's da scoop? My old lady claims that I need more fiber in my diet. I say once a week is fine for me, but she says I'm too, uh, ya know, uh ... anyway, I'm no refined kind of guy, see, but I love my refined foods. You can say they made me what I am today. Constipated, yeah that's it, that's what my wife called me. So what's the real story? Do I need to eat this brown rice sh...stuff or what?

Meat and Potatoes

Dear Meat,

Thanks for sharing a universal concern. Hopefully we can flush away your confusion and relieve your, uh, doubts. Too much refined food wreaks havoc with that colossal colon of yours. Manly men, such as yourself, need the heavy cleansing action that only high fiber foods can provide. This includes brown rice, whole grain breads, fresh fruits and vegetables, (is this a broken record that's playing?) beans, nuts, and seeds. Try a little at a time and see if that doesn't improve your ... whole entire life.

Dear Delia and Polly,

I have recently grown concerned about the risks of eating foods sprayed with pesticides. I would normally relate risk taking to indulging on banana splits, over charging on my husband's credit card, or even leaving a clay mask on for too long; but in this case I am referring to toxic chemicals that I am ingesting with my food. Just how dangerous to myself and my family is eating this way?

Risk Taker

Dear Risky,

We're impressed with the brash, daring, audacity of your risk taking and bow to your living life so close to the edge; however, you probably don't realize how close to the edge of real danger eating foods sprayed with pesticides is taking you and your family.

You would swoon if you knew how many different chemicals are used on our foods today. Herbicides, pesticides, and fungicides cover a broad spectrum of the applied poisons. These chemicals vary tremendously in their immediate toxicity, how long they persist on food, in the water and ground, as well as their carcinogenic properties. When you add to this picture the fact that many crops have more than thirty different chemicals approved for use on them, you can see that trying to accurately assess the impact on your health is very difficult.

Merely placing a ban on the use of certain chemicals is of little use. Certain chemicals such as DDT have been banned in the Unites States yet continue to be sold to foreign countries for use on their crops. Some of these crops are then exported to the United States, distributed to our supermarkets, and end up on your plates. In a Senate Agricultural Committee hearing in September 1991 concerning the sale of these banned poisons it was revealed that 1.2 million pounds of chlordane, 150,000 pounds of Dicofol, and 1.2 million pounds of Mirex had been shipped from American ports to foreign countries.

Some of the chemicals used on our crops are carcinogenic. This is particularly a problem for children who are more susceptible to the effects of these poisons. Despite the evidence the use of toxic pesticides on our food continues.

The destruction that these poisons also cause to the environment is far reaching and devastating. Some chemicals which are very toxic but break down quickly in open air and sunlight last much longer when they are mixed into the soil. Pesticides and chemical fertilizers are continuously leached in great quantities into our soil and water.

This in turn has a drastic effect on all of the rest of the ecosystem that comes in contact with those chemicals. Rivers, oceans, and underground water supplies are contaminated, the soil is depleted of vital nutrients, and the whole balance of the natural environment is disrupted.

It all sounds pretty bleak but there are some things that you can do about this problem. Washing your produce well can help reduce the amount of agricultural sprays you are ingesting. Support organic farmers by buying their products. This will help insure that more organically grown food will continue to be available. Ask your local grocer to stock organic food whenever possible. Let them know that there are concerned consumers shopping at their store. Most importantly, consider becoming a vegetarian. A 1981 study showed that vegetarian women had much lower levels (98% less) of certain pesticides in their breast milk than the national average.[1]

These are some of the ways you can care for yourself and your families health. Good Luck!

Dear Delia and Polly,

I never though I would be writing to you but what has happened is so unusual that I needed to talk to someone about it. Recently, while ridding my refrigerator of mystery leftovers turned blue ribbon science experiments, I steeled myself before opening the fruit and vegetable drawer. Courageously I pulled the drawer open and to my surprise I found two week old strawberries still fresh and unblemished. It frightens me to think what must have been done to them in order for them to keep this long. They do look good and I am tempted but are they harmful for me to eat?

Strawberry Fields Forever

Dear Fields,

Those strawberries may have been around forever and still look good enough to eat, but you may be shortening your own shelf life by eating foods that have been irradiated. In a nutshell, irradiation involves exposing foods to very large doses of ionizing radiation from a source such as Cobalt 60 or Cesium 137, in order to increase the foods shelf life by killing unwanted bacteria and insects. Although irradiation can reduce the bacterial load on food, it does not eliminate chemical toxins that may exist from earlier contamination, and it may create new toxins in the food.

1. Hergenrather J, Hlady G, Wallace B, Savage E. Pollutants in breast milk of vegetarians. *Lancet* 1981;304:792

It is known that irradiation diminishes the vitamin content of foods, especially when high doses of radiation are used. Vitamin A, vitamins B1, B2, B3, B6, B12, folic acid, vitamins C, E, and K are all damaged to some extent by irradiation.[2] Irradiation literally changes the molecular structure of food, resulting in the formation of new chemical products, some of which are known carcinogens. These include Formaldehyde, Benzene, peroxide, Benzopyrene, and quinones.

So resist the temptation and go ahead and throw out those oh-so-fresh strawberries. In the future buy organic non-irradiated foods and eat them before they go bad. Bon Appetit!

Dear Polly and Delia,

My future mother-in-law has let me know, in her oh-so-subtle way, that my career just might interfere with my being able to feed her precious son properly. Girls, she wants to give us a microwave oven as a wedding gift. Granted, it will cut my cooking time to almost nothing and insure that Junior gets his on the table every night, however, the use of the terms "nuked" or "zapped" has raised questions in my mind as to the safety of eating microwaved food. Just what is your position on this subject.

Not Yet Zapped Bride

Dear Soon To Be Zapped,

Up until recently dear Zapped, there has been little research into the effects of eating microwaved food. However, microwaving is known to have a definite effect on the molecular structure of food.

The problems from microwaves fall into two basic categories. The first is damage to cells from direct exposure to microwaves. This can happen when microwave ovens leak. The second is a result of eating food that has been altered by heating with microwave radiation.

If you insist, however, on using a microwave then buy a leak detector so you can check regularly to insure there is no leakage from your oven. Better still, refuse to be a guinea pig for this latest experiment of modern technology. Why risk sacrificing the health of yourself and loved ones for a few quick meals. Use this book instead and see for yourself just how little time it takes to prepare healthy, delicious meals.

2. Tommy Webb, Tim Lang, Kathleen Tucker, *Food Irradiation, Who Wants It?*, Thorsin's, Vermont, 1987, 156 pages

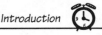

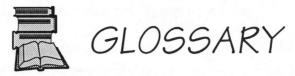

GLOSSARY

Amazake - A sweet beverage made from sweet brown rice. Available in health food stores.

Arrowroot - A natural thickener made from the arrowroot plant. Dissolve the arrowroot in a small amount of cool liquid before adding to sauces, gravy, pies, or puddings.

Bragg Liquid Aminos - A seasoning liquid made from vegetable proteins.

Brown Rice Vinegar - A mild, delicious vinegar made from brown rice. Don't be fooled by grocery store varieties of "seasoned" rice vinegar - sugar is added.

Carob - Made from the pods of the carob tree, carob is used as a substitute for cocoa powder, but unlike chocolate it contains no theobromine (a caffeine-like substance) or oxalic acid. It's high in minerals, low in fat, and naturally sweet, so less sweeteners are needed in baking. Carob is available toasted or untoasted, in powder, chips, or block form. There are dairy-free and sugar-free chips available.

Falafel Mix - A traditional, Middle Eastern mix made from seasoned chick-peas, rolled into balls and fried.

Hummus - Another Middle Eastern dip made from chick-peas, garlic, lemon juice, and tahini.

Lentil Pilaf - Brown lentils and rice with seasonings added.

Mirin - A traditional Japanese sweet rice wine seasoning. Used in marinades, salad dressings, noodle broths, or to mellow out salty or overly spiced foods. Look for naturally brewed varieties.

Miso - A paste made from soybeans with barley or rice added, water, sea salt, and koji (a cultured rice mold). Miso aids in digestion and is most commonly used to flavor soups, sauces, and spreads.

Nutritional Yeast - A food yeast grown on a molasses base. It contains all the essential amino acids, is a good source of protein and B-vitamins, comes in yellow flakes or powder form, and tastes great.

Rice Flour - A fine flour made from brown rice. Good for cookies, crusts, and quick breads.

Soba Noodles - A Japanese noodle made from buckwheat flour.

Soy Cheese - A non-dairy alternative to cheese with the same melting properties and similar taste. Soy cheeses come in cheddar, jalapeño, and mozzarella varieties.

Soy Mayonnaise - You guessed it, a non-dairy mayonnaise with its roots in the soybean field. Available in health food stores.

Soymilk - A non-dairy alternative to cow's milk made from soybeans. Available in original, vanilla, and carob flavors. Can be used as cow's milk for drinking or cooking. Also available in low-fat varieties.

Soysage - A vegetarian alternative to sausage made from the magical soybean and spices.

Spelt flour - Flour made from the spelt grain, an ancient grain of the wheat family, yet wheat sensitive people seem to be able to tolerate this distant cousin.

Spike - A dry seasoning mix of herbs, with or without salt, available in both grocery and health food stores.

Tahini - A nut butter made form ground sesame seeds. Tahini comes in raw and roasted varieties.

Tamari / Shoyu - Good quality Japanese soy sauces. Aged in wooden kegs for 2 years, tamari is wheat-free. Shoyu has wheat and has a mellower taste. Also available in "low-sodium" varieties. Substitute 2-3 parts tamari or shoyu for 1 part salt in recipes.

Tempeh Burger - A prepared, frozen burger patty made from fermented, seasoned soybeans. Similar in texture to beef burgers.

Tofu - A high protein food made from soybeans. Curdled much the same way cottage cheese is curdled and then pressed. Tofu is very versatile to cook with.

Tofu Scrambler - A seasoned, nutritional yeast-based powder mix. Add to crumbled, sautéed tofu for a scrambled egg substitute.

All of the mixes listed in the glossary are readily available at your health food store. Some grocery stores carry falafel and lentil-pilaf mixes.

Shopping

Having wandered the aisles of grocery stores from Florida to Maine to Washington state, (don't we sound like fun), we have found some chains much more hip than others as to just what they consider healthy and saleable. The truth of the matter is, if you want something, THEN ASK FOR IT! Go to the manager, show him the name of the product manufacturer, and say, "My money wants to buy this item. Please order it for me." It's that simple, ladies and gentlemen. You are the power behind the throne, so tell them what you want, be OBNOXIOUS and bingo! healthy food at your fingertips. We have made a general list of what you can expect to find in the grocery, health, and oriental food stores.

This list is not to say that you can't buy most of these items in a health food store as well. However, if you're looking to do one-stop-shopping with occasional foraging elsewhere, then your grocery store will do just fine.

Where we live, in Sarasota, Florida, we are very fortunate to have a large and thoroughly stocked natural foods store. Yet we found a Kroger's grocery store in a small town in Tennessee that had an extremely large section of natural foods products. In Seattle the organic blue chips are on the shelf next to the Fritos, while next to Newman's Own was a well-stocked macrobiotic section. As my mamma once told me, "You better shop around, ohhh baby, ya better shoooopppp around."

Things are looking up though. In practically every grocery's produce section, nestled between the bean sprouts and the bok choy, is the "What the heck do I do with you" tofu. FLASH WARNING ... DO NOT, WE REPEAT, DO NOT EAT THIS PRODUCT PLAIN OUT OF THE PACKAGE. Our advice to you first timers is to pick a recipe that appeals to you from this book (so many tofu recipes, so little time), prepare the tofu according to the recipe (very important!), and then enjoy this wonderful and nutritious high-protein food.

My Momma said,
"You'd better shop around."

SUPERMARKET	HEALTH FOOD STORE	ORIENTAL STORE
frozen veg/fruits	soy sauce	coconut milk
canned beans	bread	curry paste
olive oil	nuts	
fresh veg/fruits	seeds	
instant rice	tempeh	
cereal	bean cakes	
sweetener	tahini	
tofu	almond butter	
canned soup	soy cheese	
rice cakes	soymilk	
ethnic foods	sweeteners	
pasta	muffins	
nuts	crackers	
tea	dried fruit	
corn chips	cookies	
corn tortillas	**BOXED MIXES:**	
fruit juice concentrate	Tofu Scrambler	
apple sauce	Lentil Pilaf Mix	
dried mushrooms	Hummus Mix	
jarred vegetables	Burger Mix	
salad dressings	soy mayonnaise	
vinegar sauces	soysage	
jams	Frozen Beancake	
peanut butter	whole wheat pizza crust	
herbs/spices		
vanilla		
flour		
sea salt		
sake		
whole wheat pita		
chopped nuts		
muffins		
crackers		
dried fruit (pieces)		
cookies		

The "One Foot In The Kitchen" Pantry

Discovered in an ancient cave dwelling. Here is a letter from a mother to her newly married daughter.

If you have any intention of cooking these recipes, you're going to need the following utensils:

Blender: You'll use this a lot for sauces and creams. To speed the cleaning process, put a cup of water in the blender immediately after using, and blend.

Food Processor: This one need not be too big a machine in order to get the job done—slicing, dicing, pureeing, chopping, shredding, and mixing.

Juice squeezer: For a quick squeeze job on those lemons and limes.

Large skillet: A good iron skillet is a must have and can handle any cooking job. We even bake in ours. Stainless steel is excellent as well, but try to avoid the teflon coated aluminum pots and pans. The jury is still out as to just how much of the pots and pans you're eating with your food, and how it can adversely affect your health.

Saucepans: Stainless steel, enamel, or glass will do fine.

Steamer: A definite for quick and easy cooking. Ask Santa for a stainless steel pasta pot with the inner strainer, along with that cute little silk teddy you've been wanting. They both can double for any number of things.

Oven and range: Just try cooking without one; unless, of course, you're into wood stoves just like grandma used to use. Actually, gas and wood are the best for cooking with.

Toaster Oven: When it's just you and the cats for supper, this is the fastest way to go. Also, when it's just nuts or bread that need toasting ... gee, that's why they call it a toaster oven!

Microwave Oven: Although the great majority of Americans feel blessed to have this contraption in their kitchen, we do not share their enthusiasm. If you insist on using yours however, then do so carefully and with an eye always on the possibility of it leaking radiation. Check it on a regular basis with a microwave leakage detector and have it serviced if anything seems unusual. There are still many studies being done on the safety of microwave cooking. Are Americans the guinea pigs for these tests? Don't sacrifice your health for a quick meal. Use this book instead and you'll find that you don't need that old microwave after all.

EXTRAS:
    Measuring cup and spoons
    Very sharp knife
    Mixing bowls in several sizes
    Wooden spoon for stirring
    Garlic press
    Grater
    Baking tray
    Large Cutting Board

Everything Your Mother Never Told You About ... Herbs

Discussions of what herbs to use when preparing Tofu Scrambolito or just what herbs make up the French Blend have never been big in mother-daughter, heart-to-heart talks. Like some other heart-to-hearts our mothers never quite got around to. Though you may not learn any more about sex from this book, we will, at least, fill in the gaps on herbs and just how to handle THEM.

Using the right herbs, individually or in combinations, can turn an ordinary, bland dish into something special and delicious. It takes little or no extra effort and the results are fantastic. (Not bad for little or nothing). Experimenting with herbs to find tastes you like is very important. However, the most important thing is that you do not use the herbs that have been on your pantry shelf for the last 4 years. Throw them out! Start fresh! Buy only what you need from the health food store (they sell in bulk quantities), and store them in airtight jars. If you use them on a regular basis then store them on the pantry shelf. If, however, you buy black mustard seeds for a particular East Indian chutney and know you won't use them again in the near future, then label them (so you won't mistake them for roach doo-doo), and store them in the freezer.

You can buy herbs in tins and jars at any grocery store. These work fine although you pay a lot more for packaging. It is imperative that you have certain herbs available in your kitchen, and we have made a list of what you'll need to get started. Making your own herbal blends can be less expensive, and you make only what you can use.

KITCHEN HERBS (Individuals)

basil	onion	paprika	coriander
oregano	garlic	cardamom	mint
cumin	sage	black pepper	cayenne
thyme	dill	chili powder	
bay leaf	tarragon	allspice	
cinnamon	marjoram	ginger	

HERBAL BLENDS

La Cucaracha
Mexicali Blend
2 Tablespoons chili powder
1 Tablespoon cumin
1 Tablespoon oregano
1 Tablespoon garlic
1 Tablespoon sea salt

The Big Easy
Cajun Blend
1 Tablespoon chili powder
1 Tablespoon paprika
1 Tablespoon onion flakes
1 Tablespoon allspice
1 ½ teaspoons cayenne
1 Tablespoon thyme

Ah Mama Mia!
Italian Blend
1 Tablespoon garlic
1 ½ Tablespoons basil
1 Tablespoon thyme
1 Tablespoon oregano
1 Tablespoon rosemary
½ Tablespoon marjoram
½ Tablespoon sage
1½ teaspoons red
    pepper flakes

Simple Italian Blend
1 Tablespoon oregano
1 Tablespoon basil
1 Tablespoon thyme
½ Tablespoon marjoram
1 Tablespoon rosemary

Oooh La La
French Blend
2 Tablespoons rosemary
2 Tablespoons thyme
1 Tablespoon savory
1 Tablespoon basil

Curry Blend
3 Tablespoons curry
    powder
2 Tablespoons cardamom
1 Tablespoon black pepper

Scrambler Mix
1 teaspoon turmeric
1 teaspoon cumin
1 teaspoon curry powder
4 teaspoons onion powder
4 Tablespoons nutritional
    yeast
4 teaspoons chives
4 teaspoons dried parsley
teaspoon sea salt

When substituting fresh herbs for dried herbs, use three times the amount of fresh. This also depends on how strong the herb is. For example: 3 teaspoons fresh herbs = 1 teaspoon dried.

Canned Soups

Conspicuously absent from our line-up of recipes is the any-port-in-a-storm meal from a can. Soups are notorious for coming in handy in all kinds of situations. Because they are so easy to prepare, we will devote only a few well chosen words to them. We both learned early in life, as we climbed hand over hand up our mothers' skirts to see just what the secret ingredient was in everything she fed us, that low and behold – it was canned soup. Need a sauce for chicken, hamburger, or noodle bake – you guessed it – soup.

It may well be that you bought this lexicon of culinary gobble-de-gook (our book) because you were tired of cooking with canned soup and wanted some fresh ideas as to what to feed the clamoring hordes. We look at it as an exercise in creative imagination or cooking from both sides of the brain. A can of soup in the left hand, the refrigerator door in the right. Here's our quick overview:

Uses: Soups, sauces, casseroles, binders, stir-fries, chili, and pot-luck dinners. Use them over pasta instead of a marinara or Alfredo sauce. Add more vegetables, tofu, or tempeh to make a hearty stew. Combine cooked noodles, vegetables, and beans with your favorite soup in a casserole pan, and bake for 20 minutes. Change the noodles to a cooked grain, use a different soup, and presto! another casserole.

It's not something you want to do for every evening's meal, mind you, but it is a change from the usual pizzas and the fast food joints.

Prepare Ahead Of Time

We can already hear the groans starting as you read the heading to this chapter. "I thought this was supposed to be a quick and easy cookbook. Are these actually going to take some time?"

Yes, dear chef and chefette, this will take a little extra time but will save you countless hours and money in the days to come. Prepping your own beans, grains, and baking mixes will save you the cost of fancy packaging and give you fresher, more nutritious food as a whole.

If the idea is totally repulsive to you, quickly turn the page. If you give it a try and it doesn't prove to be worth the time and effort, then tear this chapter out of the book and light your grill with it. At least look it over and imagine that you will actually prepare these recipes ahead of time so that they will be at your fingertips just when you need them most (every day).

Don't panic and think that you have to pre-mix all these recipes at one time. Otherwise, we'll have to retitle this The Endless Food Prep Cookbook. Buy the ingredients and when you're ready to bake a cake or cookies, even pancakes, just make the extra amount these mixes call for, and you'll have them for many days to come. We tried it and it's great!

BAKING MIXES

Both the grocery and health food stores offer cake and cookie mixes that contain an assortment of ingredients that you may or may not want in your final product. If you're trying to switch to a higher quality sweetener, then it serves you well to prepare your mixes ahead of time, seal in individual zip lock bags, label, and store in the freezer.

1. CAKE, MUFFIN, PAN BREAD MIX   (Makes 4 bags)
5 cups whole wheat flour or spelt flour
5 cups unbleached white flour or rice flour
1½ teaspoons sea salt
2 Tablespoons non-aluminum baking powder
1 Tablespoon baking soda

Combine all ingredients thoroughly. Scoop 2½ cups per zip lock bag, and store in the freezer until ready to use.

2. PANCAKE MIX OR CORNBREAD (Makes 4 bags)
5 cups whole wheat flour or spelt flour
5 cups corn meal
2 Tablespoons non-aluminum baking powder
1 teaspoon salt

Combine thoroughly. Scoop 2½ cups per bag, zip, freeze.

3. COOKIE, CRISP, CRUST (Makes 3 bags)
3¾ cups oats
2½ cups whole wheat flour or Spelt flour
¾ teaspoon sea salt
2 teaspoons cinnamon
1¼ cups almonds, chopped very fine

Place the oats and almonds in a food processor, and grind to a coarse consistency. Combine in a bowl with the other ingredients. Scoop out 2½ cups per bag, and store in the freezer in individual zip lock bags.

Cooking Dried Beans And Peas

Eating beans gives you enough gas to reach the moon, you say? Well, that's an energy source well worth looking into for our space program, but we venture to guess that this unwanted personal energy output ... putt ... putt is due to 2 main reasons: 1. The beans were improperly cooked, and 2. You ate too darn much of them!

In regards to #2, eating too big a serving of beans, properly cooked or not, can cause upset if you aren't accustomed to eating beans as your main source of protein. The body actually needs time to adjust to this high-fiber, low-fat protein bean. Start with, or cut back to, ¼-½ cup servings, and then gradually increase the portions as your intestines allow.

As for reason #1, below is an important checklist for preparing these bountiful beanies so they'll be easily and quietly digested.

1. Sort through beans (throw out large branches and rocks) and rinse.

2. Soak large beans* overnight in 3 times the amount of water (refrigerate in warm weather, leave on countertop in cool weather).

3. Drain off soaking water and cook with fresh water.

4. Cook with bay leaf (European style), slice of fresh ginger root (Chinese style), or a 3-6" piece of kombu seaweed (yes, seaweed) Japanese style.

5. Bring to a boil for 5 minutes, reduce heat, skim off any foam, cover, and gently boil until soft.

6. NEVER salt beans until after they're cooked or else their skin will be tough and that means what? "They'll be hard to digest!" Right!

BEANS (1 cup dry)	WATER (cups)	BOILING TIME (minutes)
Aduki	4	60
Black Turtle *	4	90
Black-eyed Peas	3	60
Chick Peas (Garbanzos) *	4	90
Kidneys *	3	90
Lentils	3	45
Limas *	4	90
Navy	3	60
Pintos	3	80
Soybeans	4	Pressure cook only (1 hour)
Split Peas	3	60

*large beans

P.S. You cannot cook a bean too long. The longer you cook them, the mushier they become, the easier to digest, the closer to the earth you'll stay (see opening line, this section).

P.P.S. Cook more than you need, and freeze the rest for quick prep time, next time.

Cooking Whole Grains

We have both discussed this and we think that you're old enough to know where Wonder Bread comes from. Let's see ... ahem ... well, when two whole grains love each other very much ... Alright, enough of this silliness. The truth is, the whole grain, wheat berries in particular, are ground to a flour, the bran is sifted out, the flour is then bleached and stripped of any remaining nutrients, some lab-produced nutrients are added back in ("forti-fied" they call it), the dough gets conditioners, preservatives, chemicals, and a long list of other additives and voila: gut glue. Now wouldn't you like to know what a whole grain tastes like before it is so unjustly abused? Here's a quick how-to chart:

* Rinse grains to wash off dust and foreign particles.

* Add water or stock and a pinch of sea salt before cooking to make them what? "More digestible!" Right!

* Bring to a boil, cover, lower heat, and simmer for recommended time.

* NEVER stir cooking grains. This makes them sticky and clumpy.

GRAIN (1 cup dry)	WATER (cups)	COOKING TIME (minutes)
Amaranth	3	25
Barley	2¼	60
Brown Basmati	2	45-50
Millet	2½	30
Rice		
Short Grain	2½	50
Medium Grain	2	45-50
Long Grain	2	45-50
Sweet	2½	50
Wild	2	50
Quinoa	2	20
Bulgur	2	15
Couscous	2, boiling	5-10

P.S. Make more than you need, and use the rest for adding to soups, salads, and morning puddings.

BREAKFAST

 Indicates recipes that take 15 minutes or less to *prepare and cook!*

SINCE YOU'RE UP.........

Up at 5:00 A.M. doing yoga breathing exercises while feeding the cat. Milk goat, grind wheat, make 4-course breakfast. Huh, what? Oh, must have been dreaming again. Or else that was a previous life flashback. Does a quick cup of coffee and a handful of Cheerios sound more like it?

Well, WE'RE not going to mention anything about early birds catching the worm, being healthy, wealthy, and wise, you know, life's irritatingly wise little ditties. WE'RE just going to offer you some recipes and breakfast ideas so tempting you'll want to set your alarm 10 minutes earlier in order to have plenty of time to enjoy them.

Apple Harvest

3 Servings
Prep: 5 minutes
Cook: 10 minutes

1½ cups water
1 cup wheat, rye, or rice flakes, or oatmeal
¼ teaspoon sea salt
½ cup vanilla soymilk
1 cup applesauce
½ cup fresh dates, chopped, or date pieces
¼ cup almonds, chopped,
    or 1 (1 oz) package slivered almonds

Bring water to a boil. Add grain and salt. Cover, reduce heat, and simmer until liquid is absorbed (about 10 minutes). Stir in remaining ingredients and serve.

Per Serving: Calories: 315, Protein: 9 gm., Fat: 9 gm., Carbohydrates: 50 gm.

Peanut Honey Crisps

4 Servings
Prep: 5 minutes
Cook: 10 minutes

A sweet way to start the day that will keep you energized all morning.

3 Tablespoons nut butter (peanut, sesame, or almond)
3 Tablespoons low-fat granola
3 Tablespoons honey

6 slices whole grain bread
2 large bananas

Mix together first three ingredients. Spread evenly on bread. Cut bananas in half crosswise, then slice each half lengthwise into four slices. Place two slices on each piece of bread. Place side by side on a baking sheet, and drizzle with honey. Broil until lightly toasted.

Per Serving: Calories: 269, Protein: 7 gm., Fat: 8 gm., Carbohydrates: 43 gm.

Tofu Vegetable Scramble

4 Servings
Prep: 10 minutes   Cook: 10 minutes

As a power breakfast or a Sunday brunch, all this dish calls for is a side helping of your favorite bread and enough time to appreciate the flavors.

1 Tablespoon toasted sesame oil
½ red onion, chopped
1 clove of garlic, minced, 1 teaspoon pre-minced
    garlic, or ½ teaspoon garlic powder
½ red pepper, chopped, or ¼ (8 oz) jar of roasted
    peppers
1 lb tofu
½ cup water
1 (1.35 oz) package tofu scrambler or ⅓ cup
    Scrambler Mix (see page 22)
2 cups fresh Swiss chard or spinach, chopped
½ cup soy cheese, grated (optional)

Sauté onion, garlic, and pepper in oil until tender. Crumble tofu into vegetables and stir well. Add water and scrambler mix, and combine thoroughly. Add greens and stir. Sprinkle grated soy cheese on top, cover, and reduce heat to simmer. Cook five more minutes or until the cheese has completely melted.

Serve with toasted wheat bread.

Per Serving: Calories: 206, Protein: 16 gm., Fat: 12 gm., Carbohydrates: 7 gm.

Clark Kent 5-Grain

 Prep: 3 minutes
Cook: 6 minutes

Dessert for breakfast anyone? That plain, drab, hot cereal you've been avoiding is really SUPER CEREAL in disguise.

1 SERVING	2 SERVINGS	4 SERVINGS
2 Medjool dates	4	6
or 3 teaspoons date pieces		
¾ cup water	1½ cups	3 cups
⅓ cup 5-Grain Cereal*	⅔ cup	1½ cups
¼ teaspoon orange extract	½ teaspoon	1 teaspoon
¼ teaspoon vanilla extract	½ teaspoon	1 teaspoon
pinch of cinnamon	¼ teaspoon	½ teaspoon
½ cup soymilk	1 cup	2 cups
or light amazake beverage		

Remove the seeds from the dates, and place them with the water in a small saucepan. Bring to a boil and add the cereal, extracts, and cinnamon. Reduce the heat and simmer for 5 minutes. Turn off the heat, cover, and go finish dressing. Spoon into a bowl and pour the soymilk or amazake over the cereal.

Top with sliced banana, other fruit or nuts, and seeds.

* **5-Grain cereal** is a pre-toasted, quick, hot breakfast cereal consisting of rice, rye, wheat, triticale, and oats. 5-Grain alternatives – cream of wheat, muesli, or any hot quick cereals.

Per Serving: Calories: 201, Protein: 9 gm., Fat: 4 gm., Carbohydrates: 31 gm.

Cashew French Toast

3 - 4 Servings
Prep: 12 minutes   Cook: 8 minutes

Calories? Who's counting? This is well worth the indulgence!

¾ cup water
½ cup raw cashews
3 pitted dates
pinch sea salt
½ teaspoon vanilla
½ teaspoon cinnamon

6 slices whole grain bread
2 teaspoons vegetable oil

Place first five ingredients in a blender, and puree until smooth. Place bread slices in baking dish, and pour the pureed mixture over them. Allow to soak 5 to 35 seconds depending on the density of the bread, then turn and soak other side for 5 to 35 seconds. Lightly oil a skillet and heat. Place bread in pan and cook until brown; turn and brown on other side. Serve with fruit jam or pure maple syrup.

Variations: Instead of cashews use ¼ cup tahini, ¼ cup almond butter, or ¼ cup peanut butter, and replace dates with ½ ripe banana.

*Per Serving: Calories: 288, Protein: 8 gm., Fat: 14 gm.,
Carbohydrates: 32 gm.*

Banana Mash

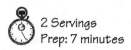 2 Servings
Prep: 7 minutes

Here is a cholesterol-free alternative to cream cheese, and it's more satisfying.

1 large ripe banana
¼ cup nuts of choice, chopped
1 Tablespoon nut butter of choice
1 Tablespoon raisins
2 cinnamon raisin bagels or 2 slices of nut bread

Mash banana with a fork. Fold in remaining ingredients and spread on a cinnamon-raisin bagel or nut bread.

Per Serving: Calories: 464, Protein: 13 gm., Fat: 14 gm., Carbohydrates: 69 gm.

Sweet Wrap

 1 Serving
Prep: 5 minutes
EAT: 5 minutes

Put that donut down and mash this together instead.

¼ cup soft silken tofu
1 Tablespoon nut butter (peanut, almond, cashew, or sesame)
1 Tablespoon sweetener (maple syrup, rice syrup, honey, or barley malt)
¼ cup raisins or chopped dates
1 round of pita, or chapati bread, or whole wheat tortilla

Mix first four ingredients together well, and stuff it in the pita bread as you close the door behind you.

Per Serving: Calories: 398, Protein: 12 gm., Fat: 10 gm., Carbohydrates: 64 gm.

Rice Cream Deluxe

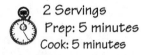
2 Servings
Prep: 5 minutes
Cook: 5 minutes

Now read it again slowly: RRRRice Cream Deluxe, not Ice Cream

½ cup Quick Cooking Rice Cereal
2 cups water
1 teaspoon vanilla extract
1 teaspoon orange extract
pinch of cinnamon

Toppings: tupelo honey, toasted nuts, fresh or dried fruit, soymilk or amazake beverage

Bring water to a boil, add extracts and cinnamon, and whisk in rice cereal. Simmer for 2 minutes, turn off heat, and allow to sit for 5 minutes while you finish shaving. Place rice cereal in a bowl, and top with tupelo honey, toasted nuts, and fresh or dried fruit. Pour soymilk or amazake over it all, and wake up with a smile.

If you don't have rice cereal you can use, cream of wheat, or ⅔ cup rolled oats

Per Serving (with toppings): Calories: 243, Protein: 7 gm., Fat: 3 gm., Carbohydrates: 46 gm.

Captain Crisp

Makes 12 cups
Prep: 10 minutes

*This is a sorta Do Ahead recipe, because you make a lot of it
ahead of time, but it's well worth it. You can use it for cereal,
toppings, dessert cookies, or straight from the jar at snack time.
Ideal!*

1 (8 oz) box or 6 cups unsweetened puffed grain
    cereal of choice: Kashi puffed cereal or a
    combination (2 cups each) of puffed cereal such
    as wheat, corn, and rice
½ cup each: almonds, walnuts, sesame seeds, and
    pumpkin seeds, chopped and roasted
2 cups raisins
2 cups dried fruit: date pieces, apricots, apples,
    etc.
2 teaspoons cinnamon

Obtain a large jar to store the cereal. Meanwhile, combine all
ingredients in a large bowl, and sprinkle with cinnamon. Mix
thoroughly, scoop into the jar, and store.

*Per Cup: Calories: 324, Protein: 6 gm., Fat: 11 gm.,
Carbohydrates: 47 gm.*

Breakfast Muesli

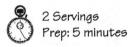

2 Servings
Prep: 5 minutes

You may not buy boxed cereal again. Cold soymilk is the key to flavor here. This can be easily doubled or tripled to have extra on hand.

1 cup rolled oats
1 cup wheat germ
¼ cup raisins
2 - 4 Tablespoons wainuts, almonds, or sunflower
   seeds, chopped

2 cups soymilk or more to taste
1 apple, pear, or any fruit in season

Coarsely chop first four ingredients together in a food processor with several on/off pulses. Place in a bowl and pour cold soymilk over it. Allow to soak while you chop the fruit into bite-size pieces. Add the fruit and chew slowly.

*Per Serving: Calories: 626, Protein: 32 gm., Fat: 20 gm.,
Carbohydrates: 78 gm.*

Hothot Couscous Cerealcereal

2 Servings
Prep: 3 minutes
Cook: 5 minutes

Can you boil water? Maybe?
Well then, even you can make this yummy breakfast.

1 cup couscous
1 cup vanilla soymilk
2 Tablespoons maple syrup

Bring all ingredients to a simmer over medium heat, and stir until thick. Top with raisins or nuts, and serve with extra soymilk.

Per Serving: Calories: 271, Protein: 9 gm., Fat: 2 gm.,
Carbohydrates: 54 gm.

Gooey Grape Nuts

1 Serving
Prep: 6 minutes
EAT: TAKE YOUR TIME

The origin of this recipe? I thought the applesauce was soymilk
in those dark morning hours. What a great mistake!

½ cup grape nuts
unsweetened applesauce
2 Tablespoons nuts, chopped
dash of vanilla

Add just enough applesauce to all of the above to create a gooey consistency you'll really, really love. Serve in a bowl as is, or spoon over a toasted bagel.

Per Serving: Calories: 335, Protein: 9 gm., Fat: 9 gm.,
Carbohydrates: 56 gm.

Vegetable Pancakes

Makes 12 large pancakes
Prep: 20 minutes   Cook: 20 minutes

1 (10 oz) package soft silken tofu
3 cups water

Use Cake, Muffin, Pan Bread Mix # 1 (see page 25), or mix in a large bowl:

2 cups whole wheat flour
2 cups cornmeal
2 rounded teaspoons non-aluminum baking powder

1 teaspoon each: basil and tarragon
½ teaspoon each: oregano and sea salt

2 medium carrots
1 medium zucchini
¼ small butternut squash
½ onion, minced

Grate the vegetables by hand or in a food processor, and set aside. Blend together tofu and water. In a large bowl, mix flour, baking powder, and spices. Whisk the wet mixture into the dry. Mix completely until smooth, and fold in the vegetables. Don't over mix. Lightly oil a frying pan, and heat oil over medium heat. The pan is ready when a drop of water hops and sizzles across the surface. Pour into the pan two cakes at a time. Brown on both sides. Serve with Lemon Tahini Sauce (see page 129).

Can be frozen for next weekend's lazy Saturday morning

Per Pancake: Calories: 184, Protein: 6 gm., Fat: 1 gm.,
Carbohydrates: 35 gm.

Brown Rice Puddin'

4 servings (½ cup each)
Prep: 5 minutes   Cook: 20 minutes

This breakfast makes you feel loved, somehow.
Also good cold as a dessert.

1 cup quick brown rice, uncooked, or 2 cups cooked
    brown rice
½ cup apple juice
¾ cup vanilla soymilk
½ teaspoon cinnamon
¼ cup raisins
pinch of sea salt
Toppings: honey, maple syrup, or fruit preserves,
    chopped walnuts

Combine all ingredients in a medium saucepan. Slowly bring to a boil over medium heat. Lower heat and simmer until almost all liquid is absorbed, about 15 minutes.

Drizzle with honey, maple syrup, or fruit preserves, and top with chopped walnuts. Toasty to your toes!

Per Serving: Calories: 236, Protein: 4 gm., Fat: 3 gm.,
Carbohydrates: 48 gm.

LUNCH

How To Prepare Tofu

Have you run out of ideas as to what to do with tofu? Have you ever had a good idea as to what to do with tofu? Well, we've had five and here they are.

But first, a word from our sponsor:

Tofu is such a bland food—not unlike Aunt Estelle—yet it's considered to be the Lawrence Olivier of healthy foods—versatile and chameleon-like, that is. With proper make-up and costume, tofu can be transformed into an award winning dish—like Liz.

One thing you can do is marinate it, so that when you're ready, it's ready to perform—pickled and seasoned, sort of like Dean Martin.

Let it sit in the fridge until you get up the nerve to use it (or until your next mortgage is due, whichever comes first). Now come on, just do it and you'll like it. EAT YOUR TOFU, you knucklehead. Now go to your room!

    1 lb tofu
    1 cup water
    ¼ cup soy sauce
    juice of one lemon
    1 clove garlic or ½ teaspoon minced garlic orgarlic
        powder

Slice the tofu into ¼" slabs, place them in a pyrex dish, and cover with mixture of water, soy sauce, lemon, and garlic. Store in the fridge or use right away. When ready to use, pan fry with 1 Tablespoon of oil, or cut into cubes and add to a stir-fry at the end of the vegetable cooking time.

 Indicates recipes that take 15 minutes or less to *prepare and cook!*

Tofuna or
What The Heck Is It?

4 Servings
Prep: 10-15 minutes

½ lb firm tofu
2 stalks celery, finely chopped
¼ cup onion, minced
¼ cup tahini
2 teaspoons tamari
2 Tablespoons nutritional yeast
¼ cup lemon juice

Using a potato masher, combine all ingredients until mixed thoroughly. Serve a scoop over fresh greens, or use as a spread on the bread of your choice with tomato, avocado, and sprouts.

Per Serving: Calories: 163, Protein: 8 gm., Fat: 9 gm.,
Carbohydrates: 9 gm.

Tofu Tarragon

4 Servings
Prep: 10-15 minutes

½ lb firm tofu
1 stalk celery, finely minced
¼ cup roasted red pepper, chopped
1 scallion, chopped
2 Tablespoons lime juice
1 Tablespoon + 1 teaspoon low-fat soy
    mayonnaise
½ Tablespoon dried taragon
Herbamare salt to taste

Crumble tofu into a bowl, and add the other ingredients. Mix well and serve in pita pocket, over fresh greens, or between two slices of French bread.

Per Serving: Calories: 60, Protein: 4 gm., Fat: 3 gm.,
Carbohydrates: 3 gm.

Curried Tofu Spread

 4 Servings
Prep: 10-15 minutes

½ lb reduced-fat tofu
¼ cup peanut butter
2 teaspoons cider vinegar
1 rounded teaspoon curry powder
1 Tablespoon + 1 teaspoon tamari
1 Tablespoon honey
2 Tablespoons peanuts, chopped (optional)

Using a potato masher combine first six ingredients, adding the peanuts last. Serve on a pita, with greens and vegetables, between two pieces of whole wheat bread, or spread on celery and cucumber sticks.

Per Serving: Calories: 145, Protein: 8 gm., Fat: 8 gm.,
Carbohydrates: 8 gm.

Oriental Tofu Stix

 4 Servings
Prep: 10-15 minutes

½ lb firm tofu
2 scallions, chopped
3 Tablespoons toasted sesame seeds
1 small carrot, grated
½ can water chestnuts, chopped
⅓ cup Mahvelous Marinade (see page 133)

Slice the tofu into ¼" x 2" sticks. Combine with the other ingredients in a mixing bowl, and toss well. Serve with norimake slices (vegetarian sushi), over fresh napa and bok choy greens, or with cold soba noodles and chilled, steamed broccoli.

Per Serving: Calories: 100, Protein: 5 gm., Fat: 6 gm.,
Carbohydrates: 7 gm.

Sun-Dried Italian Tofu

4 Servings
Prep: 10-15 minutes

½ lb firm tofu
1 cup water
1 Tablespoon soy sauce
5 sun-dried tomatoes
12 toasted almonds, sliced or slivered (optional)
2 Tablespoons red onion, minced
2 Tablespoons fresh parsley, minced, or
    parsley flakes
½ teaspoon dried basil
1 teaspoon olive oil
2 teaspoons balsamic vinegar
Herbamare salt to taste

Preheat oven to 350°F. Cut the tofu into small cubes. In a small saucepan, bring water and soy sauce to a boil, and add the tofu. Reduce heat to simmer and cook for 6 minutes, stirring occasionally. Meanwhile, soak dried tomatoes in enough hot water to cover. Place the almonds on a baking sheet, and toast in the oven for 6-8 minutes. Chop the onion and parsley while the almonds are toasting. Drain the tofu. Drain the tomatoes and chop fine. Place the tofu and all ingredients in a mixing bowl, and toss well. This is delicious with greens, steamed vegetables, cold pasta, or in a pita pocket with lettuce.

Per Serving: Calories: 87, Protein: 5 gm., Fat: 3 gm.,
Carbohydrates: 9 gm.

Sandwiches
Pseudo Greek

2 Servings
Prep: 10 minutes

1 cup Tofuna (page 44)
1 pita, sliced in half
½ cup roasted red pepper, chopped
5 Greek olives, chopped
2 lettuce leaves or sprouts

Open the pita halves half way. Stuff with ingredients and watch them disappear.

Per Serving: Calories: 342, Protein: 14 gm., Fat: 13 gm.,
Carbohydrates: 39 gm.

New Delhi Belly

2 Servings
Prep: 10 minutes

1 cup Curried Tofu (page 46)
1 pita, sliced in half
1 carrot, chopped fine
1 stalk bok choy, chopped
¼ cup broccoli, fresh or frozen, finely chopped
2 lettuce leaves

Lightly steaming the vegetables makes for a nice twist on this theme. Simply open the pita halves, stuff, then stuff your mouth with them.

Per Serving: Calories: 333, Protein: 15 gm., Fat: 11 gm.,
Carbohydrates: 42 gm.

Tofu L&T To Go

1 Serving
Prep: 6 minutes
Cook: 2 minutes

2 - ¼" slices tofu
oil for frying (sesame, safflower, corn, olive, or
   canola)
splash of tamari
1 thick slice tomato
2 crunchy lettuce leaves
low-fat soy mayonnaise
whole grain bread of choice

Heat a small amount of oil in a skillet over medium heat. While it's heating, pop the bread in the toaster. Slap the tofu in the skillet with a splash of tamari, fry 1 minute, flip, splash, and fry 1 minute more. Smear mayo on golden toast, and assemble tofu with lettuce and tomato. Now go!

Per Serving: Calories: 194, Protein: 9 gm., Fat: 5 gm.,
Carbohydrates: 26 gm.

Bean Burger

4 Servings
Prep: 10 minutes   Cook: 14 minutes

Way lower fat, way tastier, way better for you than moo-cow burgers.

2 cups leftover beans of any kind, (lentils,
    garbanzo, navy, kidney) drained
2 Tablespoons sesame, peanut, or almond nut
    butter (optional)
¼ cup onion, chopped, fresh or frozen
    or 1½ Tablespoons onion powder
1 Tablespoon arrowroot or whole wheat flour
2 Tablespoons spices of choice (or one of the herb
    mixtures on page 22)

Coarsely mash the beans with a potato masher or heavy fork. Mix all together, mold into patties, and fry. Top with mushroom sauce or the usual burger condiments.

*Per Serving: Calories: 170, Protein: 8 gm., Fat: 4 gm.,
Carbohydrates: 26 gm.*

Eggless Egg Salad

2 Servings
Prep: 10 minutes

½ lb firm tofu, (1 cup, crumbled)
1 stalk celery, chopped
2 rounded Tablespoons each: pickle relish, red
   onion, minced, red pepper, diced
1 teaspoon mustard
¼ cup low-fat soy mayonnaise or eggless
   mayonnaise
½ package Tofu Scrambler or ½ recipe Scrambler
   Mix (page 22)
1 teaspoon tamari
2 Tablespoons nutritional yeast (optional)

Crumble the tofu into a bowl. Add remaining ingredients and mix well. Serve in pita bread or mounded on a salad.

Per Serving: Calories: 212, Protein: 12 gm., Fat: 9 gm.,
Carbohydrates: 15 gm.

All Stirred Up

4 Servings
Prep: 12 minutes   Cook: TILL HOT

They'll think you've been over a hot stove all day
slow-simmering this one. HA!

1 package of 4 vegetable or tofu burgers, thawed
if frozen
1 (10 oz) package frozen vegetable medley, your
choice
1 (8 oz) can stewing tomatoes
1 large clove garlic, minced, or ½ teaspoon pre-
minced garlic or garlic powder
1 bay leaf
¼ cup red wine (optional, but highly
recommended)

Crumble vegetable patties into a pot with remaining ingredients, and simmer for as long as you have time for. Serve with chunky bread.

Per Serving: Calories: 241, Protein: 10 gm., Fat: 11 gm.,
Carbohydrates: 22 gm.

Tofu Quiche

4 Servings
Prep: 20 minutes   Cook: 15 minutes

Let's face it, you cannot duplicate a cheese and egg-laden pie with tofu, but it's darn close and it's awfully darn good!

1 large onion, thinly sliced
1 cup fresh or frozen, broccoli florets
1 cup mushrooms, sliced
1 cup frozen corn
1 Tablespoon olive oil
½ lb firm tofu
1 cup soymilk
pinch of nutmeg
1 teaspoon dried basil or dill
1 teaspoon sea salt
black pepper to taste
1 jalapeño pepper, chopped (optional)

Preheat oven to 325°F. Saute onion, broccoli, mushrooms, and corn in olive oil for a few minutes. Blend tofu with soymilk, herbs, and seasonings. Place vegetables into a 9" x 9" pyrex dish, and pour tofu mixture over top. Bake, uncovered, approximately 15 minutes, or until a knife inserted in the custard comes out clean.

Per Serving: Calories: 150, Protein: 7 gm., Fat: 6 gm., Carbohydrates: 14 gm.

Out Of This World

1 Serving
Prep: 10 minutes   Cook: 10 minutes

¼ cup water
½ onion, sliced into half moons
½ roasted red pepper, sliced into strips
    or ⅓ (8 oz) can red pepper
1 teaspoon toasted sesame oil
1 slice tofu (½" thick from 1 lb block), marinated
    and cut into strips (see Mahvelous Marinade
    page 133)
1 whole wheat tortilla
¼ avocado, sliced
¼ cup jalapeño soy cheese, grated

Sauté the onion and pepper in water adding small amounts to prevent scorching. When tender, remove and sauté the tofu in oil on both sides until brown. Lay out the onion, pepper, and tofu down the center of a whole wheat tortilla. Add sliced avocado and grated jalapeño soy cheese, roll, and seal with a toothpick.

Per Serving: Calories: 368, Protein: 11 gm., Fat: 23 gm.,
Carbohydrates: 28 gm.

Tortilla Flats

1 Serving
Prep: 5 minutes

1 tortilla
4 Tablespoons avocado, mashed
1 slice tofu (½" thick from 1 lb block),
    1 commercial bean cake, or ⅓ cup mashed beans
1 scallion, sliced lengthwise
1 Tablespoon commercial raspberry vinaigrette
    dressing, or rice vinegar
lettuce or sprouts

Layer on tortilla: avocado, tofu, bean cake, or beans, scallion, vinaigrette, and lettuce. Roll and devour.

*Per Serving: Calories: 246, Protein: 7 gm., Fat: 8 gm.,
Carbohydrates: 36 gm.*

Pocket Stuffer

1 Serving
Prep: 7 minutes

1 whole wheat pita (2 pockets)
2 slices tomato
1 tempeh burger, thawed to room temperature,
    cut in strips
¼ green pepper, sliced, fresh or roasted
4 cucumber sticks, sliced
prepared mustard of choice
2 lettuce leaves

Lightly toast the pockets. Slice open and stuff them with the other ingredients. Put your feet up, pop a cool one, and chew slowly. Life is good!

*Per Serving: Calories: 259, Protein: 13 gm., Fat: 5 gm.,
Carbohydrates: 40 gm.*

Cool Chili

6 Servings
Prep: How long does it take you to open a can?
Cook: How long does it take your stove to heat a pot of chili?

1 (16 oz) can kidney beans
1 (16 oz) can tomatoes
1 (16 oz) can tomato sauce
5 oz frozen corn (½ of 10 oz package)
1 cup frozen chopped onion
1 envelope chili mix or 2-3 Tablespoons MexicaliMix
    (page 22)
¼ cup cornmeal

Mix. Heat. Eat.

*Per Serving: Calories: 151, Protein: 6 gm., Fat: 0 gm.,
Carbohydrates: 30 gm.*

Apple-Almond-Miso Spread

 2 Servings
Prep: 5 minutes

2 Tablespoons almond butter
¼ cup apple butter
2½ teaspoons miso
2 Tablespoons water
slivered almonds (optional)

**Mix all ingredients and enjoy on rice cakes or crisp bread for a
snack-type lunch.**

*Per Serving: Calories: 191, Protein: 3 gm., Fat: 9 gm.,
Carbohydrates: gm.*

Far East Sandwich Feast

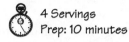

4 Servings
Prep: 10 minutes

Please don't ignore this exotic spread. Check out the glossary to understand the ingredients, then check out the smile on your face when you try it.

½ cup mellow white miso
½ cup tahini
1 small onion, diced
1 large carrot, grated

Mix all together in a bowl. Spread thinly on your favorite bread and top with tomato and cucumber slices.

*If you have a food processor, this recipe can be done in the working bowl. Shred carrot first, replace disc for blade, and pulse chop the onion. Add miso and tahini and blend just until mixed.

Per Serving: Calories: 251, Protein: 8 gm., Fat: 15 gm., Carbohydrates: 20 gm

Chick-Pea and Flee

4 Servings
Prep: 12 minutes

A great sandwich filling. Also good as a spread for crackers,
or as a dip for vegetables.

1 (16 oz) can chick-peas (garbanzo beans)
2 Tablespoons tahini
2 Tablespoons commercial vinaigrette dressing
½ cup carrot, zucchini, yellow squash,
   or spinach, grated
2 Tablespoons lemon juice or rice vinegar

Drain peas and mash all ingredients together in a bowl using a fork or in a food processor. Spread on bread with tomato and lettuce or sprouts.

Per Serving: Calories: 254, Protein: 10 gm., Fat: 8 gm.,
Carbohydrates: 35 gm.

Gazpacho

4 Servings
Prep: 10 minutes

We used to know a lot of people who didn't think soups should be served cold. We now know a lot of people who have changed their minds on this issue.

4 ripe tomatoes, quartered
1 small onion, coarsely chopped
1 medium cucumber, peeled and coarsely chopped
1 clove garlic, peeled
1 cup tomato juice
2 Tablespoons lemon juice
salt and black pepper to taste
cayenne to taste
1 sprig fresh parsley, destemmed
4 ice cubes

Toss everything into a blender or food processor, and blend until vegetables are small but not pureed. Season to taste. The ice cubes add a little water as they melt, and help to chill the soup.

*Per Serving: Calories: 55, Protein: 2 gm., Fat: 0 gm.,
Carbohydrates: 11 gm.*

1, 2, B B Q

4 Servings
Prep: 8 minutes   Cook: 30 minutes

This'll satisfy your hankerin' fer some barb-y-que.

1 lb tofu, diced
1 lb fresh or frozen broccoli, chopped small
1 large onion, diced, or 2 cups frozen onion
¾ cup barbecue sauce

Mix together and bake in a 9" x 9" casserole in a 350°F oven, covered, for 30 minutes.

Per Serving: Calories: 219, Protein: 12 gm., Fat: 5 gm.,
Carbohydrates: 31 gm.

Refried Rollups

4 Servings
Prep: 10 minutes

These have become a staple in our lunch boxes. Vary it week to week with different beans. Just mash and wrap.

4 corn or whole wheat tortillas
1 (16 oz) can vegan refried beans
½ cup fresh or frozen corn
⅓ cup mild salsa
1 large lettuce leaf

Combine the beans with the corn and salsa. Spread on a tortilla, top with the lettuce leaf, roll it up, and munch.

*Per Serving: Calories: 260, Protein: 11 gm., Fat: 2 gm.,
Carbohydrates: 49 gm.*

Ramen On The Run

2 Servings
Prep: 7 minutes
Cook: 5 minutes

1 cup water
1 (3 oz) package ramen noodles (omit flavoring
    package)
1 cup fresh or frozen vegetables, chopped
    (peppers, carrots, summer squash, cabbage,
    scallions, or whole peas)
⅓ cup firm tofu, cubed
1 Tablespoon tamari
1 Tablespoon peanut butter (optional)
dash hot sauce (optional)

In a medium saucepan, bring the water to a boil. Add the noodles, stirring with a fork to separate them, and reduce heat to medium. Stir in the vegetables and cook for 3 minutes, until the noodles are separated but still firm. Drain off any remaining water. While still hot, stir in the tamari, peanut butter and hot sauce, if desired. Serve warm, room temperature, or chilled.

*Per Serving: Calories: 245, Protein: 9 gm., Fat: 10 gm.,
Carbohydrates: 29 gm.*

The Californian

1 Serving
Prep: 7 minutes

Ally Sheedy really, really loved this one. Oh, yeahh, really.

2 slices hunky whole grain bread (sprouted or
    sourdough)
Dijon style mustard
¼ ripe avocado
1 thick slice sweet onion
1 thick slice tomato
1 hefty handful of sprouts
2 Tablespoons vinaigrette dressing

Spread one piece of bread with mustard. Cut avocado in thin half moon slices, and lay out atop mustard. Top with onion, tomato, and sprouts, and sprinkle with vinaigrette dressing. Cap it off with the remaining slice of bread, and slice in half to enjoy your artistry.

*Per Serving: Calories: 244, Protein: 7 gm., Fat: 9 gm.,
Carbohydrates: 32 gm.*

Pinto Bean Salad

2 Servings
Prep: 10 minutes

1 (16 oz) can pinto beans, drained and rinsed
½ small onion, minced
2 stalks celery, thinly sliced
1 small carrot, shredded
¼ cup favorite pickle relish
¼ cup low-fat soy mayonnaise

Combine all ingredients in a bowl, and mix well. Serve on a bed of lettuce with our own Cheese Muffins (page 63) as a side nosh.

*Per Serving: Calories: 245, Protein: 10 gm., Fat: 6 gm.,
Carbohydrates: 53 gm.*

Vegetable Cheese Muffins

Yield: 12 muffins
Prep: 15 minutes   Bake: 20 minutes

3 cups whole wheat flour
½ cup cornmeal
2 Tablespoons baking powder
½ teaspoon salt
½ teaspoon thyme
1½ cups water
½ cup sweetener (honey, maple, or rice syrup)
¼ cup vegetable oil
½ cup each: carrot and zucchini, shredded
2 Tablespoons fresh or frozen onion,
    finely chopped
½ cup cheddar soy cheese, shredded

Preheat oven to 375°F. Mix dry ingredients in one bowl and wet ingredients in another. Mix together and add the vegetables and cheese. Spoon into oiled muffin tins, and bake for 20 minutes.

*Per Serving: Calories: 226, Protein: 5 gm., Fat: 6 gm.,
Carbohydrates: 37 gm.*

Cold Sesame Noodles And Vegetables

4 Servings
Prep: 20 minutes   Cook: 8 minutes

Leftover noodles and veggies are perfect for this recipe.

1 (8 oz) package Chinese soba noodles
2 cups fresh or frozen broccoli, chopped
2 cups fresh or frozen cauliflower, chopped

SAUCE:
In a blender puree:
⅓ cup tahini
1-2 cloves garlic or
½ teaspoon pre-minced garlic
1" peeled fresh gingerroot or 1 teaspoon
powdered ginger
½ cup apple juice
juice of one lime
2 Tablespoons tamari or Bragg Liquid Aminos
½ cup water
pinch of cayenne

Bring 2 quarts of water to a boil to cook noodles. Just before they are tender, about 5 minutes, add the vegetables for the remainder of the cooking time. Drain and cool to room temperature or colder. Toss the noodles and vegetables with the sauce, and serve with a salad.

Per Serving: Calories: 320, Protein: 10 gm., Fat: 11 gm., Carbohydrates: 46 gm.

Quick Cold Lunch From Leftovers

2 Servings
Prep: MINIMAL
Cook: NONE

More often than not there will be certain leftovers that will sit in the fridge until their odor propels you to pitch them, all the while feeling guilty for wasting perfectly good food. Or you can do something ingenious and transform last night's dinner into this afternoon's feast.

1. PASTA SALAD
    To 2 cups leftover spaghetti (plain, without sauce) add:
    ⅓ cup red onion, finely chopped
    ½ cup canned corn
    ½ cup red pepper, chopped
    ½ cup celery, chopped
    fresh parsley, chopped
    vinaigrette dressing of choice

Combine all ingredients in a bowl, and toss with a tart vinaigrette dressing.

Per Serving: Calories: 219, Protein: 7 gm., Fat: 1 gm., Carbohydrates: 46 gm.

2. LEFTOVER VEGETABLES: ALL SOUPED UP
2 cups raw or cooked vegetables
¼ cup Pesto Sauce (page 134)
¼ cup silken tofu or soymilk
1½ cups water
2 Tablespoons tamari

Place ingredients in blender, blend together, and serve chilled or at room temperature in soup bowls along with crackers or bread.

Per Serving: Calories: 219, Protein: 7 gm., Fat: 1 gm., Carbohydrates: 46 gm.

3. BEAN SPREAD/FILLING
To 1 cup leftover lentils (or any bean, or any bean/grain combo) add:
½ cup celery
⅓ cup red onion, chopped
1 clove garlic, minced
1 small tomato, chopped
salt to taste

Combine ingredients in a food processor, and puree until smooth. Roll up in a whole wheat chapati with lettuce, or use to stuff a pita pocket.

Per Serving: Calories: 141, Protein: 7 gm., Fat: 0 gm., Carbohydrates: 27 gm.

Memories of youth recall school lunch bags containing two pieces of Wonder Bread, margarine, and a slab of bologna. All right, so it was more than the starving children of China had, but you still couldn't have convinced me to eat it. What we know now about nutritious meals and what was known then are worlds apart in taste and satisfaction. This is a sure fire way to win your child's or spouse's complete devotion, at least until lunch is over.

Sandwich Mix And Match

Bread	Spread	Vegetable	Condiments
Pita	Hummus	Red onion	Mayonnaise
Tortilla	Tofu burger	Avocado	Mustard
Chapati	Grain burger	Tomato	Ketchup
Hoagie	Tempeh burger	Cucumber	Salad dressing
Foccacio	Bean cake	Lettuce	Lime juice
French	Bean spread	Sprouts	Lemon juice
Kaiser roll	Tofu salad	Pepper	Marinnaise
Croissant	Soy cheese	Pickle	Bragg Aminos
Thin-Thin	Peanut butter		Fruit jam
Muffins	Almond butter		Apple butter
Biscuits	Sesame butter		Honey
Slices			

Pick the BREAD ... lay it out.

Pick the SPREAD ... spread it.

Pick the VEGETABLE ... slice and lay.

Pick the CONDIMENT ... top it all.

Open your MOUTH ... eat it.

DINNER

PIZZA

Pizza has become America's grand ole dame; the staple food on which she lives. When touring the country, we noticed that there was never a lack of pizza or ice cream parlors, regardless of the size of the town or city or its inhabitants. Whether ordering out or buying ready-made in the grocery freezer, pizza is the All-American, quick and easy meal. With that in mind, we've developed some pizza recipes that will provide more than just dough and cheese: a full meal in a slice. Accompanied by a tossed green salad, all you need do is push the remote control with your toe and settle down in front of the tube again.

Now in order to insure that we would reach a variety of palates, we decided to have a party. A pizza party, where everyone brought their favorite pizza toppings, pre-made pizzas, or pizza crusts, and we each created our own signature pizza. Of course, it was vegetarian toppings we requested, and yet some hard core carnivores were intent on smuggling in a round of pepperoni and sausage. It's real hard to change those old habits and food patterns, especially when it concerns an individual's favorite pizza toppings. Everyone agreed to put aside their cows and pigs for the evening and try their creations à la vegetarian. Ta Da! Success after success. The pizzas were delicious. We overdosed on dough and soy cheese, but what the heck! Each of us came away happy and convinced that our own was the best tasting creation.

Here are five of the recipes for you to try, or, if you wish to create your own signature creation, follow the easy mix and match pizza chart (page 73) and enjoy the all-time, American pastime—eating pizza.

A few general tips to know when assembling pizza from scratch: All the ingredients listed in the recipes should be layered beginning with the sauce and working your way up from there. Frozen pizza crust is easy to lift and can be cooked on the oven rack. Otherwise, place the crust on a round pizza pan or flat cookie sheet. Use caution when transferring the pizza from the oven to the cutting board, or you could very well be scraping your signature pizza off the kitchen floor.

 Indicates recipes that take 15 minutes or less to *prepare and cook!*

THESE SERVE FROM 1-4 PEOPLE ... FESS UP!

Bake each pizza in a pre-heated 400°F oven
for 12-15 minutes

David's Simplicity

1 10" whole wheat pizza crust
1 (8 oz) jar pizza or spaghetti sauce
garlic, chopped
¼ cup black olives, chopped
¼ cup green peppers, chopped
⅛ cup canned chili peppers
Italian plum tomatoes, sliced
1 cup mozzarella soy cheese, grated

Per ¼ Pizza: Calories: 302, Protein: 9 gm., Fat: 16 gm.,
Carbohydrates: 32 gm.

Dan's Classic Gourmet

1 10" whole wheat pizza crust
1 (8 oz) jar pizza or spaghetti sauce
garlic, chopped
½ cup artichoke hearts, chopped
¼ cup black or green olives, chopped
¼ cup roasted red peppers, chopped
1 cup mozzarella soy cheese, grated

Per ¼ Pizza: Calories: 296, Protein: 9 gm., Fat: 16 gm.,
Carbohydrates: 30 gm.

Polly's Greek Island

1 10" pre-cooked, thick pizza crust or
    Foccacio bread
olive oil to brush top of bread
1 large unpeeled eggplant
1 large onion, chopped, or 1½ cups chopped frozen
    onion
1 Tablespoon oil of your choice
1 cup Tofu Cheese (see recipe below)
2-3 cloves garlic, chopped

Grill eggplant by cutting into ¼" rounds and brushing each round with olive oil on both sides. Broil on both sides 6" from heat until each side is slightly browned and soft (approximately 6 minutes on each side). Sauté onion and garlic in oil until soft (approximately 6 minutes).

Per ¼ Pizza: Calories: 236, Protein: 10 gm., Fat: 8 gm.,
Carbohydrates: 32 gm.

Delia's Meal In A Slice

1 commercial rice crust pizza
¼ cup Pesto Sauce (page 134)
1 cup fresh or frozen broccoli florets, lightly
    steamed
¼ cup roasted red peppers
½ cup Tofu Cheese (see page 72)

Tofu Cheese

½ lb firm reduced-fat tofu, crumbled
1 Tablespoon mellow white miso

Mash miso with tofu and allow to set out on the counter 1 hour before using. If you have no time, use immediately.

South Of The Border

1 10" commercial soy cheese pizza
½ can refried beans (no lard, please!)
¼ cup black olives, chopped
¼ cup green peppers, chopped
¼ cup canned chili peppers
more pizza sauce
½ cup jalapeño soy cheese, grated

After this one bakes, top it with fresh guacamole or sliced avocado and Tofu Sour Cream (see page 128).

Per ¼ Pizza: Calories: 380, Protein: 11 gm., Fat: 18 gm., Carbohydrates: 41 gm.

Pizza Mix And Match

Prep: 10 minutes   Cook: 12-15 minutes

Pre-heat the oven to 450°F. Start with the crust first, then the sauce, and finally the toppings, or reverse the order for something altogether different.

Crust	Sauce	Toppings
commercial crust	pizza	soy mozzarella
commercial pizza	spaghetti	soy jalapeño mozzarella
English muffins	salsa	onions
boboli	homemade	garlic
foccacio	olive oil	olives
French bread	none	peppers
		artichokes
		mushrooms
		refried beans
		broccoli
		sun-dried tomatoes
		zucchini
		spinach
		tofu cheese
		anything you want

A final note on home pizza creations is that **if all else fails**: time, inclination, motivation, lack of ingredients, then the following recipe is for you:

1. Go to the phone.

2. Dial your favorite pizza parlor.

3. Order the vegetarian works.

4. Listen to them freak out when you order no cheese.

5. Pop a brewsky, change into something with no waistband, and make a quick salad.

6. Answer the door, pay the boy, and settle down for a meal from which you won't easily get up.

7. Wake up in the chair at 3:00 in the morning to the T.V. test pattern and drool on your chin. Have a nice day.

Red Lentil Stew

4 Servings
Prep: 10 minutes   Cook: 30 minutes

1 cup red lentils
3 cups water or vegetable stock

1 medium onion, chopped
1 stalk celery, sliced
1 cup fresh* unpeeled butternut squash, washed,
    and cut in ½" cubes
1 bay leaf

½ cup fresh parsley, coarsely chopped
1 teaspoon sea salt or 2 Tablespoons tamari
2 teaspoons salt-free seasoning of your choice

Rinse and drain lentils quickly in cooking pot, and immediately add the water or stock. (If you move slow with these babies, they'll clump together like women gossiping at a tea party.) Add next 4 ingredients and bring to a boil. Cover, reduce heat to medium-low, and simmer for 20 minutes. Add remaining ingredients and more water if necessary. Continue to simmer another 10 minutes and adjust seasonings to taste. Serve to a Hunk ... uh, serve with a hunk of bread, yeah, yeah, that's what I meant, a hunk of bread...

*Per Serving: Calories: 207, Protein: 12 gm., Fat: 0 gm.,
Carbohydrates: 38 gm.*

***Fresh butternut** gives the dish a sweetness that frozen squash doesn't have.*

NOTE: *Wondering what to do with the remaining butternut squash? Instead of conducting a "How Quickly Will It Mold?" experiment, chop the remaining squash and steam it for 15 minutes until tender. Eat as is, toss into grain, bran, or veggie salad, sprinkle with maple syrup, mash and spread on toast ...*

Here's a recipe that can be done one of two ways, Polly's way or Delia's way. It's the same recipe with one being more elaborate than the other. When the in-laws call and say they're coming for dinner or there's a certain someone you wish to impress with your culinary expertise then we recommend this dish for a most successful dining affair. No pun intended.

Tofu Mushroom Stroganoff I

4 Servings
Prep: 10 minutes   Cook: 15 minutes

1 Tablespoon toasted sesame seed oil
1 large onion, chopped, or 1½ cups chopped frozen onion
1½ lbs mushrooms, sliced
1 Tablespoon tamari
3 Tablespoons mirin or white wine
1 (10 oz) package soft silken tofu
juice of 1 lemon
1 lb wide noodles, cooked al denté
fresh parsley for garnish, chopped

In a saucepan, heat the oil and sauté the onion until soft, 3-4 minutes. Add the mushrooms and tamari, stir, reduce heat, and cover. Allow to cook for another 3-4 minutes so the mushrooms can release their juices. Uncover and add the mirin or white wine, stir, and recover. Puree the tofu with 3 Tablespoons of the mushroom liquid, 3 Tablespoons of water, and lemon juice. When smooth, add the tofu to the mushroom mixture, and simmer for 10 minutes. Spoon over the cooked noodles, and sprinkle with chopped parsley.

Per Serving: Calories: 316, Protein: 14 gm., Fat: 7 gm., Carbohydrates: 46 gm.

Tofu Mushroom Stroganoff II

4-6 Servings
Prep: 15 minutes   Cook: 20 minutes

1 Tablespoon vegetable oil
1 large yellow onion, chopped
1 small red pepper, cut in strips
¾ lb mushrooms, sliced
3 Tablespoons whole wheat flour
¾ cup water
3 Tablespoons tamari
black pepper to taste
1½ Tablespoons fresh dill, chopped
1 lb wide fettucini noodles, cooked al denté

Tofu Sour Cream

1 lb soft reduced-fat tofu
1 Tablespoon vegetable oil
1½ Tablespoons lemon juice
2 scallion bulbs
1 teaspoon sea salt

In a saucepan, heat oil and sauté onions and red pepper until soft, about 3 minutes. Add mushrooms with a pinch of salt, cooking until they release their liquid. Add flour, stir, and continue cooking for 2-3 minutes longer, until the flour has absorbed all of the liquid. Add water a little at a time, stirring constantly to blend well. Simmer 10 minutes covered. Add tamari and pepper, and cook for 5 more minutes.

Blend all sour cream ingredients in a blender until smooth. Stir into onion mixture and add dill. Remove from the heat, adjust the seasoning to taste, and serve immediately over noodles.

Per Serving: Calories: 283, Protein: 13 gm., Fat: 9 gm., Carbohydrates: 36 gm.

American Goulash

4 Servings
Prep: 10 minutes   Cook: 15 minutes

*OK, kids, leave your school lunch money at home. Here's the
healthy replacement for that cafeteria favorite.*

1 Tablespoon safflower or canola oil
1 medium onion, chopped
1 (16 oz) can crushed tomatoes
1 medium zucchini, cut into ½" cubes,
    or 1 (12 oz) package frozen broccoli pieces
1 teaspoon oregano
1 teaspoon sea salt, 2 teaspoons tamari, or
    2 teaspoons Bragg Liquid Aminos
1 lb tofu, crumbled
2 cups cooked elbow macaroni
¼ teaspoon black pepper
soy cheese, grated (optional)

Sauté onion in oil over medium heat until soft. Add tomatoes,
zucchini (or broccoli pieces), oregano, and salt, and simmer for 5
minutes. Add remaining ingredients and heat through. Season to
taste. Top with grated soy cheese (optional).

Serve with garlic bread and a crisp green salad.

*Per Serving: Calories: 235, Protein: 12 gm., Fat: 7 gm.,
Carbohydrates: 27 gm.*

Lasagne With A Kick

6 Servings
Prep: 30 minutes   Cook: 30 minutes

Lasagne has become another American staple. Rather than spend all that time waiting for the noodles to cook, we said to heck with them and substituted sliced tofu instead. To our surprise, it works great and tastes delicious. Just don't try to tell your Italian grandmother it's called lasagne.

1 Tablespoons olive oil
1 onion, chopped
2 cloves garlic, minced
1 green pepper, chopped
1 (26 oz) jar Newman's Own Sockarooni
    Spaghetti Sauce, or sauce of your choice
2½ lbs firm reduced-fat tofu
2 (10 oz) packages frozen spinach
1 (8 oz) package jalapeño soy cheese

Preheat oven to 375°F. Sauté onion, garlic, and green pepper. When soft, add spaghetti sauce, and reduce heat to simmer. Meanwhile, slice tofu lengthwise into 18 pieces. Cook spinach according to package instructions, and grate the cheese. Layer everything in a 9" x 13" casserole pan: sauce, tofu, spinach, cheese, sauce, tofu, spinach, sauce, cheese. Bake for 30 minutes.

Per Serving: Calories: 467, Protein: 24 gm., Fat: 27 gm., Carbohydrates: 27 gm.

Millet Ragout Redo

6 Servings
Prep: 15 minutes   Cook: 20 minutes

Millet Ragout debuted in our first cookbook to so much acclaim that we're bringing it back, only a wee bit different this time.

In a saucepan combine:
2 cups millet, well rinsed
1 parsnip, grated or chopped
½ medium onion, chopped, or 1 cup frozen onion
1 carrot, grated or chopped and ¼ head cauliflower, cut in small pieces or peeled and chopped butternut squash, grated rutabaga, or chopped cabbage may be substituted for any of the vegetables
½ teaspoon sea salt
4½ cups water

3 Tablespoons tahini or 3 Tablespoons leftover Alfredo Sauce (page 84)

Bring all ingredients (except tahini or Alfredo Sauce) to a boil, and reduce heat to simmer for 20-25 minutes or until water is gone.

Add:
3 Tablespoons tahini or
3 Tablespoons leftover Alfredo Sauce (page 84)
Mix well.

Per Serving: Calories: 213, Protein: 6 gm., Fat: 5 gm., Carbohydrates: 36 gm.

* or use 1 (16 oz) package frozen mixed vegetables (example: carrot, cauliflower, green bean mix)

Quinoa, Leek, And Tofu Casserole

4 Servings
Prep: 20 minutes   Cook: 25 minutes

We know you know the words AND and CASSEROLE, while the rest reads like ancient Greek. Never fear. Go to the health food store and ask for a GRAIN CALLED QUINOA, an ONION CALLED LEEK, and a CURD CALLED TOFU. This one is too good to pass by!

2 teaspoons vegetable oil of choice
3 cloves garlic, minced or 1½ teaspoons pre-
    minced garlic
1 leek (greens and bulb), thinly sliced
3 teaspoons French Blend herbs (see page 22) or
    1 teaspoon each rosemary, thyme, savory
1 lb firm tofu, rinsed
2 cups cooked quinoa
2 Tablespoons tamari or shoyu (good quality soy
    sauce)
black pepper to taste
½ cup strong vegetable broth
½ cup soy cheese, grated
½ cup whole wheat bread crumbs

Preheat oven to 350°F. Cook quinoa according to package instructions. Heat oil in a skillet, add garlic and leek, and sauté until soft. Add 2 teaspoons French Blend herbs, and sauté for 1 minute more. Crumble tofu into skillet, add quinoa, and sauté for 5 minutes. Season with tamari and pepper. Oil a casserole dish and add tofu-quinoa mixture, pressing down gently. Pour broth over top and sprinkle with grated cheese. Set aside.

Toss bread crumbs with the remaining 1 teaspoon herb blend. Spread bread crumbs over the top of the casserole. Cover and bake 20 minutes. Uncover and bake 5 minutes longer, or until bread crumbs are lightly browned.

Per Serving: Calories: 375, Protein: 19 gm., Fat: 14 gm., Carbohydrates: 41 gm.

Broccoli Tofu Calcutta Pie

4 Servings
Prep: 10 minutes   Cook: 30 minutes

Could be mistaken for a lemon cream pie, so warn the late night fridge raiders, or a taste surprise is sure to ensue. Nonetheless, a real eye-pleaser and taste bud tantalizer. Leftovers for lunch!

1 lb firm tofu
2 cloves garlic
3 large Tablespoons peanut butter
2-3 teaspoons curry powder or
    Curry Blend (see page 22)
salt to taste
½ cup water
2 cups broccoli, chopped into small pieces, or
    2 cups frozen broccoli pieces
½ cup cashew pieces (optional)
2 cups cooked white or brown rice

Preheat oven to 375°F. Place the first six ingredients in a food processor and puree until smooth. Lightly oil a pie plate, and press the rice into the plate, keeping your fingers wet to avoid a sticky mess. If all you have is enough rice to cover only the bottom of the pie plate, that's fine. Distribute the broccoli over the rice. Pour the tofu mixture into the pie plate, top with the cashews, and bake for 30 minutes. Allow to cool for 10 minutes while you set the table, or go get the cat out of the tree.

Per Serving: Calories: 284, Protein: 14 gm., Fat: 11 gm., Carbohydrates: 32 gm.

Swing-Lo Mein

2 Servings
Prep: 10 minutes　　Cook: 10 minutes

½ (8 oz) package cooked noodles or
　2 cups cooked noodles
⅓ cup rich vegetable stock (1 bouillon cube
　dissolved in ⅓ cup hot water)
1 Tablespoon tamari
¼ teaspoon ground ginger
½ teaspoon garlic, minced
3 scallions, cut in 1" lengths
1 cup bok choy, chard leaves, or spinach leaves,
　coarsely chopped
1 cup tofu, cut in ½" cubes

Combine stock and tamari and set next to wok. Combine ginger and garlic and set next to wok. Heat wok over high heat. Add about half of the vegetable stock, all of the garlic-ginger mixture, and scallions. Stir-fry until fragrant and onions turn bright green. Then add chopped bok choy or other greens and tofu. Stir until greens are just wilted. Add cooked noodles and remaining vegetable stock. Continue stirring until noodles are heated through.

Per Serving: Calories: 267, Protein: 15 gm., Fat: 5 gm.,
Carbohydrates: 38 gm.

Black Olive Pesto

4-6 Servings
Prep: 15 minutes   Cook: 10 minutes

Want to break out of the food rut you've found yourself in? Here's a surprise that should put some zing back into your evening.

1 lb lasagne noodles, cooked
2 red peppers, cut into thin strips
8 cherry tomatoes, cut into quarters
1 handful of fresh parsley, chopped
½ lb snow peas, ends removed and steamed
    (1 minute)

Puree: (makes 2 cups of olive pesto)
Blend:
    1 cup black Greek or regular pitted black olives,
        chopped
    1 shallot, quartered
    2 cloves garlic, mashed, or 2 teaspoons pre-
        minced
    1 teaspoon basil
    1 teaspoon tarragon
    2 Tablespoons lemon juice
    ¼ cup extra virgin olive oil
    ½ cup sundried tomatoes, oil packed or
        reconstituted in hot water for 6 minutes

To serve, layer puree between cooked lasagne noodles that have been cut in half and laid out diagonally. Top with red pepper and parsley. Surround with snow peas and cherry tomatoes.

*Per Serving: Calories: 363, Protein: 9 gm., Fat: 16 gm.,
Carbohydrates: 44 gm.*

Dan's Quick

"Delia will be home any minute"

Alfredo Sauce

4 Servings
Prep: 6 minutes
Cook: 6 minutes

1 lb firm tofu
1 stalk celery
2 cloves garlic
2 Tbs Bragg Liquid Aminos or tamari
ground black pepper
2 Tablespoons tahini
½ leek
½ cup water

Place ingredients in a food processor, and puree until smooth. Use more water if you want a thinner sauce. Pour into a saucepan, and heat gently for 15 minutes. Do not bring to a boil. Serve over steamed veggies, pasta, or cooked grains.

Per Serving: Calories: 144, Protein: 10 gm., Fat: 7 gm.,
Carbohydrates: 7 gm.

Tuscany Stew

4 Servings
Prep: 15 minutes   Cook: 20 minutes

1 (16 oz) can crushed tomatoes
1 medium zucchini, chopped
1 medium onion, chopped
2 cloves garlic, minced
1 cup frozen corn
1 (10 oz) can navy beans or 1 (10 oz) package
    frozen lima beans
1 teaspoon each: basil and rosemary
1 cup Swiss chard, chopped
¼ cup white wine (opt.)
salt to taste

Combine all ingredients in a medium-sized pot. Bring to a boil, reduce heat, and simmer for 20 minutes or until the vegetables are tender.

Per Serving: Calories: 177, Protein: 8 gm., Fat: 0 gm., Carbohydrates: 35 gm.

Fettucini With Zucchini And Fresh Tomatoes

2 Servings
Prep: 10 minutes   Cook: 20 minutes

¼ lb fettucini or other pasta of choice
1 Tablespoons olive oil
2 Tablespoons water
2 small zucchini, quartered and sliced
1 cup mushrooms, sliced
sea salt
pinch of oregano
2 medium tomatoes, cubed
1 teaspoon dried basil
salt and black pepper to taste

Boil pasta according to package directions. While pasta cooks, prepare the sauce by placing oil, zucchini, mushrooms, oregano, and a generous pinch of sea salt in a skillet over medium-high heat. Sauté about 3 minutes, stirring often and adding water as necessary to prevent scorching. When the zucchini are bright green, remove from heat and set aside.

Place cooked, drained pasta back in pasta pot, and add zucchini-mushroom mixture, chopped tomatoes, basil, and salt and pepper to taste.

Toss well and serve with a hunk of whole grain bread and a salad.

Per Serving: Calories: 179, Protein: 4 gm., Fat: 7 gm., Carbohydrates: 23 gm.

Pasta Simplistico

4 Servings
Prep: 10 minutes   Cook: 12 minutes

This is a favorite, quick pasta dish that tastes like a quiet dinner in a side street cafe in Rome, Georgia ... uh, Italy. The key here is to use a good quality olive oil. If you can't smell the olives when you sniff the opened bottle, then don't waste your money.

1 lb package pasta of choice
3 Tablespoons extra virgin olive oil
3 cloves garlic, minced
1 teaspoon dried basil or 4 teaspoons fresh basil
1/4 teaspoon sea salt
1/2 cup toasted walnuts, chopped (optional)

Cook pasta according to package instructions. Sauté garlic and basil in olive oil over low heat for 3 minutes. Do not brown the garlic. Add salt and turn off heat. Set aside while the pasta cooks and the walnuts toast in the toaster oven. Drain pasta, chop walnuts, and toss with olive oil and garlic. Add salt and pepper to taste.

Per Serving: Calories: 218, Protein: 4 gm., Fat: 9 gm., Carbohydrates: 27 gm.

STOP and smell the olive oil!

Pasta Fagoli

4 Servings
Prep: 20 minutes   Cook: 15 minutes

Mamma Mia!

1 (8oz) package soba noodles or noodle noodles
2 Tablespoons olive oil
1 medium onion, chopped, or 1 cup chopped frozen, onion
3 cloves garlic, minced, or 1 teaspoon pre-minced garlic
2 red peppers, chopped, or 1 large (10 oz) jar roasted red peppers, chopped
1½ teaspoons tarragon
2 medium zucchini, chopped
1 (10 oz) can navy beans
¼ cup toasted walnuts, chopped
salt and black pepper to taste

Cook noodles according to package instructions. While pasta is cooking, sauté 1 Tablespoon oil onion, garlic, and red pepper until tender. (If using roasted red pepper wait until adding the beans.) Add tarragon and sauté for two minutes. Add zucchini, toss, cover, and simmer. Toast walnuts in the toaster oven. Add beans (and roasted peppers) to vegetables, and stir to combine thoroughly. Drain pasta and toss with one tablespoon of olive oil and chopped walnuts. Serve beans and veggies either over the pasta or on the side.

Per Serving: Calories: 303, Protein: 9 gm., Fat: 12 gm., Carbohydrates: 40 gm.

Stuffed Green Peppers

6 Servings (1 pepper per person)
Prep: 25 minutes   Cook: 20 minutes

Using the following boxed and jarred ingredients we have come up with a very good take-off on Mom's stuffed green peppers. There are different brands of instant rice and burger mixes to try. Use your favorite pasta sauce if you can't find the spicy one that we recommend—although the spice makes a difference.

1 (4.4 oz) box burger or falafel mix
6 green peppers
1 cup instant brown rice
¼ teaspoon salt
½ (12 oz) package frozen corn
1 (26 oz) jar Classico Spicy Red Pepper pasta sauce

Bring ¾ cup water to a boil. Pour over burger mix in a bowl. Let sit 15 minutes while you prepare the peppers.

Remove tops of peppers by slicing directly across the top. Save tops for later. Seed and core peppers. Invert peppers in a steamer basket, and steam for 15 minutes while you prepare the rice.

Bring 1¼ cups water to a boil, and add instant brown rice with salt. Return to a boil, reduce heat, and simmer for 10 minutes.

Remove peppers from steamer. Combine rice, burger mix, corn, and half of the jar of pasta sauce. Stuff peppers with mixture.

Remove steamer basket and water from pan. Place peppers in pan and cover with remaining pasta sauce. Add ½ cup water to bottom of pan, turn heat to low, and simmer peppers for 20 minutes.

Serve with a tossed salad and garlic bread.

Per Serving: Calories: 382, Protein: 11 gm., Fat: 10 gm., Carbohydrates: 61 gm.

Lentil Dogs

3 Servings
Prep: 30 minutes (scratch) 15 minutes (leftover pilaf)
Cook: 12 minutes

The perfect pet; quiet and clean.

2 cups cooked lentils (or lentil pilaf mix)
1 cup cooked quick brown rice
⅓ cup whole wheat flour
¼ cup walnuts, chopped (optional)
3 scallions, chopped fine
2 teaspoons tamari
¼ teaspoon black pepper
½ teaspoon thyme
1 Tablespoon oil

In a food processor, pulse-blend lentils into a coarse meal. Combine with remaining ingredients in a large bowl, working with your hands if necessary to combine thoroughly. Shape into 6 oblong patties and flatten slightly (to about ½" thickness). Heat oil in frying pan. Fry patties 2 minutes on each side until browned. Serve on toasted bread or hot dog rolls with all the trimmings.

*Per Serving: Calories: 316, Protein: 14 gm., Fat: 5 gm.,
Carbohydrates: 53 gm.*

Lentil Pâté

4-6 Servings
Prep: 10 minutes   Cook: 30 minutes

*Here is an excellent variation that bakes up into a lentil pâté to
rival any fois gras. (Fois what?)*

2 cups cooked lentils
1 cup cooked brown rice
¼ cup walnuts, chopped
3 Tablespoons Bragg Aminos or tamari
1 cup rolled oats
2 scallions, chopped
2 Tablespoons almond butter

Preheat oven to 375°F. Combine everything in a food processor,
and process until smooth. Spoon into a lightly oiled 8" x 8" baking
pan, and bake for 30 minutes. Cool and serve with crackers, rice
cakes, or as a sandwich spread or side dish.

*Per Serving: Calories: 291, Protein: 13 gm., Fat: 9 gm.,
Carbohydrates: 40 gm.*

Curried Vegetables With Pistachio Rice

4 Servings
Prep: 15 minutes   Cook: 20 minutes

This tastes as intriguingly delicious as it sounds.

1 (8 oz) can unsweetened coconut milk (1 cup)
1 cup low-fat soymilk
½ cup water
salt to taste
1-2 Tablespoons red curry paste (available in
    oriental food stores; this stuff is mean, so go
    with what your taste buds tell you)
½ cup each, chopped: cauliflower , bok choy, napa,
    carrots,
red pepper, and onion
1 (10 oz) package rice pilaf with nuts
¼ cup pistachio nuts

In a large saucepan, heat 1¾ cups coconut milk, water, and salt almost to a boil. Add red curry paste and dissolve completely. Add vegetables and cook until tender.

Meanwhile, follow package instructions for rice pilaf. When pilaf is done, stir in last ¼ cup coconut milk and pistachios. Cover and let sit until serving time.

If, by any chance, you have some of the coconut milk and vegetables left over the next day, place them in a food processor with almond or peanut butter or a handful of toasted nuts, and puree until smooth. Add more toasted nuts to thicken, if necessary, and serve as a spread for crackers or sandwiches. You can also serve it, unthickened, as a chilled soup garnished with chopped nuts and parsley. Very delicious and impressive!

Per Serving: Calories: 277, Protein: 7 gm., Fat: 16 gm.,
Carbohydrates: 23 gm.

Tofu Scrambolito

4 Servings
Prep: 15 minutes   Cook: 15 minutes

Stop! Turn down the corner of this page, run to the grocery, buy a block of tofu, and make this for dinner tonight! We bet you'll really love this one.

¼ cup water
1 large clove garlic, minced, or ½ teaspoon
  pre-minced garlic
1 medium onion, chopped, or 1 cup frozen,
  chopped onion
½ green bell pepper, chopped, or ½ cup frozen,
  chopped pepper
1½ cups button mushrooms, sliced
1 small zucchini, diced
½ teaspoon each: cumin, oregano, salt
pinch of cayenne

1 lb firm reduced-fat tofu, crumbled
½ cup water
1 (3.5 oz) package commercial tofu scrambler mix
  or ⅓ cup Scrambler Mix (page 22)
4 flour tortillas, wrapped in aluminum foil
½ avocado, sliced, cubed, or mashed
salsa

Preheat oven to 300°F. Sauté first 8 ingredients in ¼ cup water on medium heat until soft, about 5 minutes. Add tofu, water, and Scrambler Mix. Mix thoroughly and allow to simmer for a few minutes. Meanwhile, slice the avocado and warm the tortillas wrapped in foil in the oven.

To assemble: Spread tofu mixture on a tortilla, lay a couple of slices of avocado on top, spoon some salsa on top of that, wrap, and secure with a toothpick. Serve with a cucumber, radish, and romaine salad. Ole!

Per Serving: Calories: 294, Protein: 17 gm., Fat: 7 gm., Carbohydrates: 33 gm.

Mexicali Mountain

4 Servings
Prep: 15 minutes

*A layered extravaganza. Try not to have this one too often, chicita,
or your hips will resemble two giant tomatoes. Si, si!*

½ cup tofu, crumbled (4 oz)
¼ cup lemon juice
1 (16 oz) can refried beans
1 (4 oz) can chopped green chilies, drained
1 cup picante sauce
¼ cup black olives, chopped
1 bunch scallions, chopped
1 large tomato, chopped
½ cup jalapeño soy cheese, grated
1 cup Guacamole (see page 135)
1 (9 oz) bag tortilla chips

In a food processor, blend tofu and lemon juice until smooth. Add
refried beans and blend once more. Spoon mixture into a serving
dish or bowl with at least 2" sides. Evenly layer remaining ingredients one on top of each other, unplug the phone, open a cold
brewksy, turn on Andy Griffith, and dig in.

*Per Serving: Calories: 625, Protein: 17 gm., Fat: 27 gm.,
Carbohydrates: 77 gm.*

Ola! Pepper Fajitas

4 Servings
Prep: 10 minutes   Cook: 20 minutes

*Once the chopping is done, this recipe takes an occasional stirring
while the peppers get nice and soft.*

1 Tablespoons olive oil
1 large onion, thinly sliced
2 cloves garlic, minced, or 1 teaspoon pre-minced
  garlic
1 each: red, green, and yellow bell pepper, cut into
  thin strips

1½ Tablespoons Mexicali Blend (see page 22)
  or
  1½ teaspoons cumin
  ½ teaspoon each: oregano, paprika, sea salt
  1 teaspoon chili powder
  pinch cayenne
½ cup water
4 flour tortillas
shredded lettuce, chopped tomato

Sauté first 4 ingredients for 3 minutes. Add spices, stir well, and
cook another 5 minutes. Add water, cover, reduce to a simmer, and
cook until tender, about 10 minutes. Spoon mixture down the
center of the tortillas, top with lettuce, and tomato. Fold the edges
over filling. Secure with a toothpick.

*Per Serving: Calories: 189, Protein: 5 gm., Fat: 7 gm.,
Carbohydrates: 26 gm.*

Nachos

4 Servings
Prep: 10 minutes
Cook: 2 minutes

Nachos are one of those American inventions that vaguely resemble the place from whence they claim to have sprung. When we ordered these in Mexico, they rolled their eyes and told us that it was an American dish (or else, in our poor Spanish, we had asked for grits and eggs). This simple recipe couldn't be faster or easier and can be put together with leftovers or cupboard wares.

1 (12 oz) bag corn chips (try the unsalted, baked
    variety for this one)
1 (12 oz) can vegan refried beans
1 small (3 ½ oz) can chili peppers, chopped
1 (12 oz) can pitted black olives, chopped
1 (16 oz) jar salsa
2 cups jalapeño soy cheese, grated

Lay out the chips on a cookie sheet, spread the beans over them, and top with the chilies, black olives, salsa, and cheese. Broil until the cheese melts, if you can wait that long.

*Per Serving: Calories: 719, Protein: 22 gm., Fat: 38 gm.,
Carbohydrates: 72 gm.*

Burritos

2 Servings (4 burritos)
Prep: 10 minutes   Cook: 6 minutes

1 Tablespoon olive oil
½ medium onion, chopped
1 clove garlic, chopped
1 (16 oz) can refried beans
½ teaspoon cumin
salt and black pepper to taste
4 whole wheat tortillas

Sauté onion and garlic in oil, add beans and spices, and heat through.
Spoon mixture down center of tortilla, and top with choice of
guacamole, shredded lettuce, sliced olives, grated soy cheese, or
tofu sour cream. (May we recommend all of the above?) Fold edges
over top and chow down.

*Per burrito (without toppings): Calories: 280, Protein: 10 gm.,
Fat: 5 gm., Carbohydrates: 46 gm.*

Tofu Tamale Pie

*You are now approaching a recipe that will appear to have too many
ingredients for your liking. Best just skip over this one, you say to
yourself. Well, you'll notice that most of the ingredients are herbs and
spices that are losing flavor on your shelf, even as we speak. Here's a
great opportunity to show off the culinary expertise you are fast gaining
with this educational journal of health and nutrition. Albeit, quick and
easy. Trust me on this one, or is that what your "ex" once said to you?*

6 Servings
Prep: 15 minutes   Cook: 30 minutes

2 Tablespoons olive oil
1 medium onion, diced, or 1 cup frozen chopped
   onion
1 green pepper, diced, or 1 cup frozen chopped
   green pepper
3 cloves garlic, minced, or 1 teaspoon pre-minced
   garlic

1 lb firm tofu
½ cup water
1 (16 oz) can tomatoes, chopped
½ cup black olives, chopped
1 cup frozen corn
1 Tablespoon chili powder
½ teaspoon sea salt
½ teaspoon onion powder
1 teaspoon cumin
1 teaspoon oregano
1 cup corn meal

Preheat oven to 375°F. Sauté the first 3 ingredients in the olive oil
until soft. Puree tofu and water. Add remainder of ingredients and
tofu puree to the sauté, and simmer for 5 more minutes. Pour into
a lightly oiled casserole dish or large iron skillet, and bake for 25-30
minutes. It's that simple, and you thought it would take such a long
time.

*Per Serving: Calories: 249, Protein: 9 gm., Fat: 10 gm.,
Carbohydrates: 30 gm.*

Navy Bean Soup

4 Servings
Prep: 12 minutes   Cook: 20 minutes

*Here's how to make delicious soups
without ham hocks and fat backs!*

1 (12 oz) can navy beans, rinsed
1 cup water
1 cup leeks, chopped
1 cup fresh or frozen carrots, chopped
1 clove garlic, minced, or ½ teaspoon pre-minced
    garlic
1 bay leaf
½ teaspoon tarragon
salt and black pepper to taste

Combine all ingredients in a saucepan. Bring to a boil and reduce
heat to simmer for 15 minutes or until vegetables are tender. Serve
with Herbed Onion Bread (see page 137).

*Per Serving: Calories: 124, Protein: 6 gm., Fat: 0 gm.,
Carbohydrates: 24 gm.*

Millet-Lentil Stew

4 Servings
Prep: 10 minutes   Cook: 20-30 minutes

*Cut your cooking time by 15 minutes! Here's how: Soak ½ cup
lentils in about 1 cup water before you leave for work in the
morning. Drain when you get home to use in this nourishingly
yummy stew.*

4 cups water
½ cup lentils, pre-soaked
1 cup millet, rinsed
2 carrots, cut in ½" chunks, or 2 cups frozen
     cubed carrots
½ onion, chopped, or ½ cup frozen chopped onion
1 clove garlic, minced, or ½ teaspoon pre-minced
     garlic
1 stalk celery, cut in ½" chunks
2 bay leaves
1 teaspoon each: tarragon and basil
salt to taste
3 Tablespoons tahini

Add all ingredients (except tahini) to water in a large soup pot. Bring
to a boil, reduce heat to medium-low, and simmer 20-30 minutes or
until most of the water is absorbed. Turn off heat and stir in tahini,
mixing well. Serve with big chunks of sourdough bread and a crisp
salad.

*Per Serving: Calories: 478, Protein: 16 gm., Fat: 8 gm.,
Carbohydrates: 83 gm.*

Couscous Stir-Fry

4 Servings
Prep: 10 minutes   Cook: 10 minutes

*Don't panic, it only takes 5 minutes to cook the couscous.
(See grain section, page 27 for instructions.)*

2 cups cooked couscous
1 Tablespoons olive oil
½ medium onion, chopped, or ½ cup frozen chopped
  onion
1 clove garlic, minced, or ½ teaspoon pre-minced
  garlic
1 teaspoon each: dried basil and coriander
pinch of cinnamon
1 medium zucchini, chopped
½ red pepper, sliced
1 large carrot, sliced
2 Tablespoons Bragg Liquid Aminos or soy sauce
½ cup water

Cook the couscous while you prepare the vegetables. When everything is ready, heat the oil in a skillet or wok, and sauté onion, garlic, and herbs for 3 minutes. Add zucchini, red peppers, and carrots, and cook 3 minutes more. When vegetables are just tender, add couscous, Bragg Aminos or soy sauce, and water. Stir well, turn off heat, and cover until time to serve.

*Per Serving: Calories: 148, Protein: 4 gm., Fat: 2 gm.,
Carbohydrates: 25 gm.*

Stir-Fry Mix And Match (or: One Dish Delish)

Prep: 15 minutes   Cook: 6-8 minutes

Break out those rusty woks, and get ready to concoct some of the fastest and tastiest meals of your weekly repertoire. Stir-fries are the easiest way to feed the swinging single or the family of ten. Chopped vegetables (fresh or leftovers), oil, high heat, and a constant stirring action on your part can work magic over and over again. We know people who live on stir-fries and never seem to get tired of them. (YAWN!) Vary the ingredients listed to create your own signature ONE DISH DELISH!

Notes: *Vegetables are listed from longest to shortest cooking time.*

> *Be sure to chop vegetables into thin or small pieces (tiny broccoli or cauliflower florets), so everything will cook quickly.*

> *Have everything ready to go before you start because, "Oh, officer, it all stir-fried so fast! (Sob!)"*

Here We Go!

Pick an oil .... heat it high

Pick 3-5 veggies .... sauté 'em, stirring constantly (add longest-cooking veggies first with a little EXTRA LIQUID)

Pick your seasonings .... toss in and stir

Pick your extras .... (wait, let's reword that)

Pick from the extra column .... toss in, stir with a flourish

Stir in the remaining extra liquid .... stir until thickened

Serve this over rice, noodles, or anyone that strikes your fancy.

Stir-Fry Mix And Match Ingredients

Oil	Vegetables	Seasonings	Extras
peanut	onion	minced garlic	almonds
safflower	carrot	2-3 slices ginger	cashews
sunflower	corn	any listed on pages	peanuts
canola	green beans	21 and 22	tofu
	eggplant		cooked beans
	peas		
	red/green cabbage		
	bok choy stems		
	celery		
	cauliflower		
	broccoli		
	green/red bell pepper		

— — — — — — — —

yellow squash
zucchini
asparagus
snow peas

— — — — — — — —

mushrooms
bok choy greens
mung bean sprouts
spinach
chard

- - - - - - - - - - - - - - - - -

longest cooking to shortest

Extra Liquid:
   ½ cup water or veggie stock
   1 Tablespoon soy sauce
   2 teaspoons arrowroot or cornstarch

Combine and stir to dissolve arrowroot.

Mix And Match Magic

Lookit, we could spend TEN more hours making TEN more recipes, filling TEN more pages, costing you TEN more dollars OR you can mix and match your own grains, vegetables, herbs, beans, and nuts in this quick NO-TIME-NO-FRILLS chart.

For Example:

Choose from:

Column A ..... Brown rice (boil it)

B ..... Broccoli and mushroom (sauté it)

C ...... Basil and oregano (add to veggies)

D ...... Black beans (heat them)

E ...... Optional nuts and seeds, roasted*

Pile one vegetable lovingly atop the grain to create a monument to the Quick and Healthy Dinner Gods. Remember, there are no wrong answers or bad combinations.

Bon Appetit!

A	B	C	D	E
Grains	**Vegetables**	**Herbs**	**Beans**	**Nuts**
rice	broccoli	basil	black	almonds
millet	carrot	oregano	kidney	walnuts
couscous	celery	tarragon	chick peas	cashews
bulgur	spinach	dill	navy	pecans
basmati	mushroom	curry powder	lima	peanuts
barley	squash	cumin	lentils	pumpkin
oats	onion	thyme	pinto	sesame
quinoa	zucchini	French Blend	anasazi	Brazil
amaranth	cabbage	Italian Blend	adzuki	sunflower
wheat berries	kale	marjoram	split peas	
pasta of choice	Swiss chard			
	collards			
	brussels sprouts			
	bell pepper			
	leek			
	tomato			
	corn			
	parsnip			
	potato			
	asparagus			
	green beans			
	cauliflower			
	peas			

__Roasting nuts__ in the toaster oven for 8 minutes at 350°F will add a wonderful flavor to your meal. Seeds can be roasted in a dry frying pan, over a medium-low flame, stirring often.

SALADS

 Indicates recipes that take **15** minutes or less to *prepare and cook!*

A Salad

 Prep: 10-15 minutes

Any amounts and combinations of the following will make an exciting salad:

> lettuce: romaine, red leaf, Bibb, Boston, iceberg, endive
> sprouts: alfalfa, sunflower, mung bean, lentil
> celery, chopped
> carrot, shredded
> red cabbage, shredded
> tomato, chopped
> watercress
> canned artichokes (not marinated)
> daikon radish or red radish
> any leftover steamed vegetables
> cucumber, sliced
> green pepper, sliced
> onion or scallion, chopped or sliced

Toss with your favorite salad dressing, or try one of the recipes we have in this book for a quick and simple meal.

Quickie Salads

Come back from shopping and right away soak all veggies and fruits in a full sink of water with ½ teaspoon of bleach for 10 minutes. Yes, bleach! Plain, not lemon scented. This helps break down the pesticide residues clinging to the outside of the plant. No, there's no bleachy aftertaste that remains. Rinse well, pat dry, and store salad greens in a container. Also make a container of chopped broccoli, cauliflower, cabbage, and carrots, plus a container each of: chopped tomatoes and sliced onion. Then you can grab a handful any time. Also try baby carrots. They cost more, but are a great time saver.

Pasta Salad á la Fellini

4 Servings
Prep: 15 minutes   Cook: 10 minutes

To be enjoyed after a foreign flick with a glass of grape nectar.
Bellisimo!

1 (8 oz) package pasta of choice
1 (16 oz) package frozen vegetable medley

Dressing:
    1 teaspoon minced garlic
    1 Tablespoon olive oil
    1 Tablespoon water
    2 Tablespoons wine vinegar
    ½ teaspoon each: basil and oregano or
        1 teaspoon Italian Blend (page 22)
    1 teaspoon sea salt
    black pepper to taste

Cook the pasta according to package instructions. Meanwhile, mix dressing ingredients. Five minutes before the pasta is done, add frozen vegetables, and return to a boil. When the pasta is al denté, drain and run under cold water. Place pasta and veggies in a medium size bowl, add the dressing, and toss to coat evenly.

Per Serving: Calories: 159, Protein: 6 gm., Fat: 5 gm.,
Carbohydrates: 25 gm.

Educating Raita

2 Servings
Prep: 7 minutes

A raita is a cool, crisp Indian salad made with thinly sliced cucumbers or shredded carrots, yogurt, and a mild hint of spice. Since we're so enchanted with our own Tofu Sour Cream, we recommend using it.

1 large cucumber, peeled if waxed
¼ cup Tofu Sour Cream (see page 128)
½ teaspoon coriander
pinch of cayenne

Slice cucumber thin. Mix with remaining ingredients, and chill before serving.

Per Serving: Calories: 45, Protein: 3 gm., Fat: 1 gm., Carbohydrates: 5 gm.

If we could eat all plant foods raw, and properly digest them, we would probably be the most dynamic, healthy, vibrant, radiant beings on earth. For all practical purposes, though, veggie salads will have to do. Here are 5 ALIVE recipes:

Avocado Tomato Salad

2 Servings
Prep: 10 minutes

1 ripe avocado
1 ripe tomato
⅓ sweet onion, chopped
lemon juice or vinaigrette dressing

Cube the avocado and tomato, chop the onion, and place them in a bowl. Toss with lemon juice or dressing.

Per Serving: Calories: 199, Protein: 3 gm., Fat: 12 gm., Carbohydrates: 19 gm.

Oriental Sliced Salad

2 Servings
Prep: 5 minutes

1 medium cucumber, ends cut off
6" piece of daikon (Japanese radish)
1 carrot
brown rice vinegar

In a food processor fitted with the slicing blade, slice all above veggies, place in a bowl, and sprinkle with brown rice vinegar.

Per Serving: Calories: 69, Protein: 2 gm., Fat: 0 gm., Carbohydrates: 15 gm.

Sprout Salad

 2 Servings
Prep: 10 minutes

1 (4 oz) package bean sprouts
small varieties may be added raw: mung, wheat,
    sunflower seeds
larger sprouts should be lightly cooked
    (10 minutes in boiling water): chick-peas,
    aduki, lentil, green peas
1 stalk celery, chopped
¼ red onion, minced
vinaigrette dressing of choice

Toss together and chill.

*Per Serving: Calories: 32, Protein: 2 gm., Fat: 0 gm.,
Carbohydrates: 6 gm.*

Brown Rice Salad

 4 Servings (as side dish),
2 Servings (as main dish)
Prep: 15 minutes

This is a good reason to have leftover rice in the fridge.

2 cup brown rice, cooked and cooled
½ cup each: red pepper, red onion, olives, carrots,
    celery, chopped small
½ cup walnuts, chopped small (optional)
No-oil lemon vinaigrette or Italian dressing

Combine everything toss with a lemon vinaigrette dressing or even
a creamy Italian dressing, and serve on a bed of lettuce.

May be served with avocado slices on the side.

*Per Serving (serving 4): Calories: 138, Protein: 2 gm., Fat: 5 gm.,
Carbohydrates: 24 gm.*

Vegetable Slaw

 4 Servings
Prep: 15 minutes

1 medium carrot, grated
1 medium zucchini, grated

2 stalks bok choy, finely chopped

¼ head cabbage (core removed), thinly sliced
¼ red onion, thinly sliced

Combine vegetables and toss with lemon vinaigrette, eggless mayonnaise, or your favorite salad dressing.

To add a nutty flavor try adding toasted sesame, sunflower, or pumpkin seeds.

*Per Serving: Calories: 71, Protein: 1 gm., Fat: 2 gm.,
Carbohydrates: 8 gm.*

Confetti Cole Slaw

 4 Servings
Prep: 10 minutes

½ medium green cabbage, shredded
¼ red cabbage, shredded
1 small carrot, shredded
¼ cup fresh parsley, minced (optional)

1 teaspoon honey
3 Tablespoons lemon juice or apple cider vinegar
⅓ cup low-fat soy mayonnaise
salt and black pepper to taste

Shred the veggies in a food processor, one at a time. Place the prepared veggies in a large bowl. Mix the remaining ingredients with a whisk in a small bowl, and add to slaw. Season to taste and chill before serving.

Per Serving: Calories: 77, Protein: 1 gm., Fat: 3 gm., Carbohydrates: 7 gm.

Carrot Lemon Salad

 1 Serving
Prep: 5 minutes

1 large carrot, grated
juice of ½ lemon

Grate 1 large carrot with fine grater. Toss with juice of ½ lemon.

Try using sweet organic carrots for the optimum flavor.

Per Serving: Calories: 40, Protein: 0 gm., Fat: 0 gm., Carbohydrates: 9 gm.

Beet It Salad With Walnuts

2 Servings
Prep: 12 minutes

½ lb fresh beets, peeled and grated
4 lettuce leaves
½ cup parsley, chopped and loosely packed

Dressing:
   3 Tablespoons red wine vinegar
   ½ teaspoon sea salt
   ¼ teaspoon pepper
   1 Tablespoon walnut or vegetable oil
   1 Tablespoon water

Whisk the dressing ingredients together. Toss with the grated beets. Serve on top of two lettuce leaves with a sprinkle of walnuts.

Per Serving: Calories: 107, Protein: 1 gm., Fat: 7 gm.,
Carbohydrates: 10 gm.

Lentil Tabouli

2 Servings
Prep: 15 minutes   Cook: 30 minutes for lentils
CHILL: 1 HOUR

1 cup cooked lentils
2 teaspoons extra virgin olive oil
1 Tablespoon lemon juice
½ cup chopped parsley
1 clove garlic, minced
1 rounded teaspoon dried mint or 4 Tablespoons
    fresh chopped mint
¼ cup walnuts, chopped and roasted (optional)
4 scallions, chopped
salt and black pepper to taste

Combine everything and serve immediately, or chill for 1 hour to let flavors blend.

*Per Serving: Calories: 159, Protein: 8 gm., Fat: 4 gm.,
Carbohydrates: 22 gm.*

New Potato Salad

4 Servings
Prep: 20 minutes   Cook: 10 minutes

4 cups new potatoes, unpeeled, quartered
1 stalk celery, thinly sliced
2 scallions, thinly sliced (white and green parts)
⅓ cup low-fat soy mayonnaise
1 teaspoon Dijon style mustard
salt and black pepper to taste

In a medium sauce pan, add enough water to cover potatoes. Bring to a boil, reduce heat, and simmer until just tender, about 10 minutes. Drain. Combine all ingredients together in a bowl. Adjust seasonings to taste.

Per Serving: Calories: 164, Protein: 2 gm., Fat: 4 gm.,
Carbohydrates: 29 gm.

Marinated Bean Salad

2 Servings
Prep: 7 minutes   Marinate: 30 minutes (optional)

Almost as easy and MUCH better than the bean salad at your local grocery deli.

1 (12 oz) can cooked navy beans
½ (12 oz) jar roasted sweet red peppers, chopped
2 cloves garlic, minced, or 1 teaspoon pre-minced garlic
½ sweet onion, sliced in half-moons
2 hot banana peppers, sliced (optional)
¼ cup oil-free vinaigrette dressing
2 Tablespoons chopped parsley

Combine all ingredients in a bowl. For best results refrigerate for half an hour.

Per Serving: Calories: 252, Protein: 12 gm., Fat: 1 gm., Carbohydrates: 48 gm.

Mix And Match Magic

Grain Salads

We can't say enough for these quick and easy salads. Turn plain Jane grains into something very tasty and special, indeed. Use leftover or quick cooking grains to save time.

Grain	Vegetable	Dressing	Nuts/Seeds
brown rice	red onion	bottled	almonds
millet	scallion	lemon	walnuts
couscous	tomato	lime	cashews
barley	cucumber	olive oil	peanuts
bulgur	radish	vinegar:	pecans
quinoa	broccoli	raspberry	sesame
pasta	bell pepper	tarragon	pumpkin
	carrot	orange juice	sunflower
	spinach	marinnaise	
	avocado	tahini sauce	
	olives	tofu sauce	
	artichokes	pesto	
	pickles		
	cauliflower		
	sun chokes		
	sprouts		

Pick a grain .... **cook and cool it**

Pick one or more vegetables ... **chop it (them)**

Pick a dressing .... **pour it**

Pick a nut .... **date him ... uh, no .... add it**

Tossitalltogether!

SIDE DISHES, PÂTÉS, DRESSINGS, SAUCES

 Indicates recipes that take 15 minutes or less to *prepare and cook!*

Sesame Spinach

2 Servings
Prep: 10-15 minutes   Cook: 12 minutes

1 Teaspoon toasted sesame oil
2 cloves garlic, minced
1 Tablespoon sesame seeds
1 (10 oz) package frozen or ½ lb fresh spinach
salt or Bragg Liquid Aminos to taste

Cook frozen spinach according to package instructions and drain well. Fresh spinach should be washed thoroughly, dried, and chopped. Heat the oil in a skillet, and add the garlic and sesame seeds. Cook until the seeds begin to brown, then add the spinach and Bragg Liquid Aminos. Combine everything well, lower the heat, and cook until the spinach is wilted if fresh, or heated through if frozen. Turn off the heat, cover the skillet, and steam for another 3-5 minutes.

*Per Serving: Calories: 52, Protein: 3 gm., Fat: 2 gm.,
Carbohydrates: 8 gm.*

Sweet Squash

2 Servings
Prep: 5 minutes   Cook: 12 minutes

1 (10 oz) package frozen winter squash
¼ cup orange juice or ½ teaspoon orange extract
½ teaspoon vanilla
¼ teaspoon cinnamon
1 Tablespoon sweetener of your choice (optional)
pinch of sea salt
½ cup roasted walnuts (optional)

Either defrost the squash in the refrigerator overnight or cook according to package instructions, using orange juice instead of water. When the squash is hot, add the remaining ingredients and cook for 6 minutes more. Serve topped with toasted walnuts. Also delicious when combined with cooked millet and walnuts.

Per Serving: Calories: 62, Protein: 1 gm., Fat: 0 gm., Carbohydrates: 13 gm.

Green Beans Amandine

2 Servings
Prep: 5 minutes   Cook: 12 minutes

1 (10 oz) package french cut green beans
1 Tablespoon Bragg Liquid Aminos
2 Tablespoons slivered almonds

Cook beans according to package instructions. Drain and toss with olive oil. Top with slivered almonds.

Per Serving: Calories: 93, Protein: 4 gm., Fat: 4 gm.,
Carbohydrates: 10 gm.

Lively Vegetable Toss

4 Servings
Prep: 3 minutes
Cook: 8 minutes

1 (10 oz) package frozen vegetables of choice
1 Tablespoon olive oil (optional, but it tames the
    lemon juice in such a nice way)
2 Tablespoons lemon juice
½ teaspoon minced garlic

While the vegetables are cooking, mix the remaining ingredients in a large bowl. Drain vegetables, add to bowl, and toss to coat thoroughly. Serve hot.

Per Serving: Calories: 23, Protein: 1 gm., Fat: 0 gm.,
Carbohydrates: 5 gm.

Broccoli With Garlic

4 Servings
Prep: 5 minutes
Cook: 10 minutes

A side dish fit for an ex-President!

2 teaspoons olive oil
4 cloves garlic, minced
½ teaspoon hot chili pepper flakes (optional)
1 head fresh broccoli, cut in spears or
    1 (12 oz) package frozen broccoli spears

Heat oil in skillet and add garlic and chili pepper flakes. Sauté one minute and add broccoli. Toss together, lower heat, cover, and cook for 6 minutes. (Cook for 3-4 minutes if using frozen broccoli.)

Per Serving: Calories: 46, Protein: 2 gm., Fat: 2 gm.,
Carbohydrates: 5 gm.

Almond Cinnamon Rice

4 Servings
Prep: 5 minutes
Cook: 10 minutes

Here's how to blast the Boring Rice Syndrome off your table!

1½ cups instant brown rice
1 teaspoon cinnamon
1 teaspoon nutmeg
1 teaspoon sea salt
1 teaspoon canola oil
¼ cup almonds, chopped and toasted

Prepare rice according to package instructions, include the cinnamon, nutmeg, salt, and oil during cooking. Add the almonds just before serving.

Per Serving: Calories: 140, Protein: 3 gm., Fat: 6 gm.,
Carbohydrates: 19 gm.

Mushroom Pâté

8 Servings
Prep: 15 minutes   Cook: 20 minutes

Do children from rich families play pâté cake?

1 Tablespoon oil
2 medium carrots, grated
2 large cloves garlic, minced
1½ lbs mushrooms, sliced
2 onions, diced
3 (10.5 oz) blocks silken tofu
¼ cup tamari
¾ cup nutritional yeast
3 Tablespoons Worcestershire sauce
1 cup scallions
black pepper to taste

In a large sauté pan, heat oil and add carrots, garlic, mushrooms, and onions. Cook for 15 minutes on medium heat. Drain and set aside. In a food processor, process tofu, half the vegetable mixture, tamari, nutritional yeast, and Worchestershire sauce until smooth. Mix well in a bowl with remaining vegetable mixture, scallions, and pepper. Serve at room temperature or chilled, with crackers and raw vegetables.

*Per Serving: Calories: 133, Protein: 10 gm., Fat: 2 gm.,
Carbohydrates: 15 gm.*

White Bean Pâté

Yield: 1 ½ cups
Prep: 7 minutes

Mock elegance.

1 (16 oz) can cooked navy, great northern, or
    lima beans
½ cup fresh basil, loosely packed, or
    2 Tablespoons dried basil
3 cloves garlic, coarsely chopped, or
    1½ teaspoons pre-minced garlic
½ teaspoon sea salt
1 Tablespoon extra virgin olive oil
black pepper to taste

Combine in a food processor, and puree until smooth. Serve as a dip or spread.

Per 2 Tablespoons: Calories: 54, Protein: 2 gm., Fat: 1 gm.,
Carbohydrates: 8 gm.

Appetizing Caps

Prep: How many mushrooms do you plan to stuff?

10 large, firm mushrooms
1 (6 oz) tin vegetarian pâté
or use one recipe of our yummy White Bean Pâté
    to stuff 24 mushrooms

Destem mushrooms and fill caps with pâté. Garnish with parsley, watercress, finely chopped black olives, or red pepper and voilà!

Per 2 Mushrooms: Calories: 64, Protein: 3 gm., Fat: 1 gm.,
Carbohydrates: 10 gm.

Orange Miso Dressing

Yield: 1¼ cups
Prep: 5 minutes

1 cup orange juice
3 Tablespoons mellow white miso
1 large clove garlic, or ½ teaspoon pre-minced garlic
1 Tablespoon honey
1 Tablespoon brown rice, cider, or red wine vinegar
1 rounded Tablespoon chopped onion

Blend all ingredients in a blender until smooth. This dressing is great over noodle salads, cabbage slaw, or bean salads.

Per Tablespoon: Calories: 30, Protein: 1 gm., Fat: 0 gm., Carbohydrates: 6 gm.

No-Oil Italian Dressing

Yield: ¾ cup
Prep: 5 minutes

A little tart, a little spicy, a little dab'l do ya.

½ cup brown rice, red wine, or balsamic vinegar
2 Tablespoons lemon juice
2 Tablespoons prepared mustard
2 Tablespoons honey
1 clove garlic, minced or ½ teaspoon pre-minced garlic
½ teaspoon each: dried basil and oregano
salt and black pepper to taste

Whisk ingredients in a bowl, or shake in a jar with a lid for easy storage.

Per 2 Tablespoons: Calories: 30, Protein: 0 gm., Fat: 0 gm., Carbohydrates: 6 gm.

Avocado Dressing

 Yield: 1 cup
Prep: 7 minutes

¼ cup liquid of choice: vegetable stock,
    carrot juice, or water
¼ cup lime juice or lemon juice
2 Tablespoons Bragg Liquid Aminos
1 clove garlic
1 ripe avocado

Place all ingredients in a blender, and puree until smooth. Refrigerate.

Serve with salad, over grains or vegetables, or spread on bread and broil.

*Per 2 Tablespoons: Calories: 47, Protein: 1 gm., Fat: 4 gm.,
Carbohydrates: 4 gm.*

Lemon Vinaigrette

 Yield: ⅓ cup
Prep: 5 minutes

¼ cup extra virgin olive oil
juice of 2 large lemons or limes
1 clove garlic, minced
½ teaspoon basil
½ teaspoon tarragon
dash of Bragg Liquid Aminos

Place the ingredients in a jar, tighten the lid, and shake well.

*Per Tablespoon: Calories: 98, Protein: 0 gm., Fat: 9 gm.,
Carbohydrates: 2 gm.*

Dijon Vinaigrette

Yield: ½ cup
Prep: 6 minutes

⅓ cup vinegar of choice (except that horrible
   white vinegar which is good for nothing but
   scrubbing the bathroom tiles)
3 Tablespoons water
3 Tablespoons olive oil
2 teaspoons Dijon-style prepared mustard
1 teaspoon minced garlic
¼ teaspoon crushed rosemary

Combine ingredients in a jar. It is important to cover with a lid
before you shake it up good. Serve with tossed salad or with any of
the grain salads. Don't be shy. Toss those leftover cooked vegetables with it, and marinate overnight.

Per Tablespoon: Calories: 49, Protein: 0 gm., Fat: 5 gm.,
Carbohydrates: 1 gm.

Tofu Sour Cream

Yield: 1 ½ cups
Prep: 6 minutes

Believe it or not, this is a believable replacement for the real thing. Heat
gently (do not boil) if used for cooking.

1 (10 oz) package soft silken tofu
2 Tablespoons lemon juice
2 teaspoons canola or safflower oil

Blend in blender until smooth. Refrigerate what you don't use right
away.

Per 2 Tablespoons: Calories: 25, Protein: 2 gm., Fat: 2 gm.,
Carbohydrates: 1 gm.

Hummus

 Yield: 2 cups
Prep: 10 minutes

1 package hummus mix or 1 (12 oz) can chick-peas
    (garbanzo beans)
water
olive oil
juice of 2 lemons
1-2 cloves garlic
2 Tablespoons tahini

Place hummus mix or chick-peas in a food processor, add water and oil according to instructions on package. For canned chick-peas use enough water from the can to make a spreadable consistency and 1 tablespoon olive oil. Add lemon, garlic, and tahini, and puree until smooth. Chill for 30 minutes for better flavor.

Per ¼ Cup: Calories: 89, Protein: 3 gm., Fat: 3 gm.,
Carbohydrates: 12 gm.

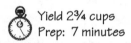

Lemon Tahini Sauce

Yield 2¾ cups
Prep: 7 minutes

Serve over absolutely any food.

1 cup tahini
1 clove garlic
1 teaspoon grated ginger
2 Tablespoons Bragg Liquid Aminos, tamari, or
    salt to taste
1½ cups water
¼ cup lemon juice

Place all ingredients in a food processor, and puree until smooth.

Per 2 Tablespoons: Calories: 64, Protein: 2 gm., Fat: 5 gm.,
Carbohydrates: 3 gm.

No Cook Tomato Sauce

Yield: 2 cups
Prep: 10 minutes

1 cup tomatoes, seeded and chopped
¼ cup mixed fresh herbs, coarsely chopped or
    ½ teaspoon each: dried herbs basil, marjoram,
    tarragon, thyme, oregano
¼ cup lemon juice or vinegar
½ small onion, minced
2-3 Tablespoons extra virgin olive oil, warmed

Mix briefly and serve over warm or cold pasta, rice, asparagus, your body, grilled garlic bread, whatever.

Per ¼ Cup: Calories: 52, Protein: 0 gm., Fat: 4 gm., Carbohydrates: 3 gm.

Roasted Red Pepper Sauce (simplified)

Yield: 2 cups
Prep: 5 minutes

Impress your friends, and yourself, with this lovely sauce.

1 (12 oz) jar roasted red peppers, with liquid
2 cloves garlic
1 Tablespoon olive oil
2 Tablespoons Bragg Liquid Aminos or salt to
    taste

Puree in a blender until smooth. Serve over veggies, grains, potatoes, or toasted bread. Dip your rice crackers in for a tasty snack.

Variation: *For "cream" sauce, add 1 (10 oz) package silken tofu. Puree until smooth. With this variation you can leave out the oil.*

Per ¼ Cup: Calories: 31, Protein: 1 gm., Fat: 1 gm., Carbohydrates: 2 gm.

Spicy Peanut Sauce

2 Servings
Prep: 5 minutes
Cook: 3 minutes

Yep - this is rich stuff.

6 Tablespoons smooth peanut butter (not freshly
   ground)
½ cup water
1 Tablespoon vegetable stock powder
1 Tablespoon honey
1 Tablespoon soy sauce
½ teaspoon ginger powder
1 teaspoon garlic
pinch cayenne

Combine all ingredients in a small saucepan. Heat until smooth and slightly thickened, 2-3 minutes, stirring frequently. Serve over grains, noodles, or steamed broccoli and cauliflower.

*Per Serving: Calories: 320, Protein: 11 gm., Fat: 21 gm.,
Carbohydrates: 18 gm.*

Basic Spaghetti Sauce

4 Servings
Prep: 10 minutes   Cook: 10 minutes - ALL DAY

We all know that no matter how good a jar of spaghetti sauce may be, it can always be improved upon. With that in mind, we present you with a quick jazz up of the spaghetti dinner recipe, sure to brighten those "Oh, no, not spaghetti again" looks at the dinner table.

1 Tablespoon extra virgin olive oil
½ onion, chopped, fresh or frozen
2 cloves garlic, minced
½ teaspoon each: dried basil and oregano
½ red bell pepper, chopped or ½ roasted red pepper, chopped
1 medium zucchini, chopped
1 (16 oz) jar of your favorite spaghetti sauce
pasta of choice
1 cup vegetable of choice (cauliflower, spinach, broccoli, etc.), chopped

Sauté onion and garlic in oil for 3 minutes, add herbs and pepper, and sauté 3 minutes more. Add zucchini and sauté until it begins to soften (about 5 minutes). Pour in spaghetti sauce, stir well, lower heat to a simmer, and cook until pasta and vegetables are done (3-5 minutes).

Cook the pasta according to package instructions, and right before the pasta is done, add the chopped vegetables and return to a boil. Cook until pasta is al denté, drain, and serve with sauce.

Per Serving: Calories: 109, Protein: 4 gm., Fat: 2 gm., Carbohydrates: 16 gm.

Tofu Sauce

Yield: 1 ½ cups
Prep: 10 minutes

1 lb firm reduced-fat tofu
3 Tablespoons tahini
1-2 clove garlic
juice of 2 lemons
½ cup water
salt to taste

Place all ingredients in a food processor, and blend until smooth.
Use more or less water depending on the consistency you want.
Great over raw salads, steamed veggies, grains, or noodles. Use less
water and serve as a dip.

*Per 2 Tablespoons: Calories: 52, Protein: 3 gm., Fat: 3 gm.,
Carbohydrates: 2 gm.*

Mahvelous Marinade

Makes 1 ½ cups
Prep: 5 minutes

½ cup shoyu soy sauce, or tamari
2 Tablespoons toasted sesame oil
¼ cup rice syrup or 2 Tablespoons honey
¼ cup cider vinegar
½ teaspoon fresh ginger juice
pinch cayenne

Whisk all ingredients together or combine in a jar and shake well.
Use as a marinade for tofu and vegetables or in stir-fry dishes. Also
great as a dressing on grains or noodle salads.

To make fresh ginger juice: Grate firm gingerroot unpeeled, on finest
grater setting. Gather the pulp in your hand, squeeze, and then
squeeze some more.

*Per 2 Tablespoons: Calories: 40, Protein: 1 gm., Fat: 2 gm.,
Carbohydrates: 4 gm.*

Pesto, The Besto!

 Makes 1 cup
Prep: 10 minutes

*Pesto is a popular Italian sauce traditionally served on hot pasta.
Other deliciouso uses are as a spread on fresh tomatoes, cooked
vegetables, and small amounts added to vegetable soups!*

1 cup fresh parsley, leaves only, lightly packed
1 cup fresh basil leaves (roughly 1 bunch), lightly
    packed
⅓ cup extra virgin olive oil
1 Tablespoon mellow white miso or ½ cup soy
    Parmesan cheese
2 cloves garlic, peeled and roughly chopped
¼ cup walnuts (optional)

Blend all ingredients in a blender or food processor to a thick paste.
Figure 1 heaping Tablespoon of pesto per serving of hot pasta. Toss
to combine thoroughly.

A convenient way to store pesto is to spoon into ice cube trays and
freeze. Defrost at room temperature. Can be kept frozen for several
months.

*Per Tablespoon: Calories: 49, Protein: 1 gm., Fat: 4 gm.,
Carbohydrates: 2 gm.*

Salsa

 Yield: 3 cups
Prep: 15 minutes

1 (16 oz) can crushed tomatoes
1 fresh tomato, chopped
½ sweet Vidalia onion (when in season), chopped
   or 1 cup chopped, frozen onions
2 cloves garlic, minced
¼ cup lemon juice
1 jalapeño pepper chopped or
   1 (4 oz) can diced peppers
dash of Texas hot sauce (optional)
salt and pepper to taste

Combine all ingredients in a bowl, and serve immediately, or chill for 30 minutes.

Per ¼ cup: Calories: 14, Protein: 1 gm., Fat: 0 gm., Carbohydrates: 3 gm.

Guacamole

 Yield: 3 cups
Prep: 15 minutes

2 ripe avocados
1 ripe tomato, chopped
½ sweet onion, chopped or 1 cup chopped frozen
2 cloves garlic, minced
juice of 3 lemons
salt to taste
dash of hot sauce or diced green chili peppers

Lightly mash the avocado and combine with other ingredients in a bowl.

Per 2 Tablespoons: Calories: 93, Protein: 4 gm., Fat: 4 gm.,
Carbohydrates: 9 gm.

Popcorn Toppings

No quick meal cookbook is complete without the indispensable popcorn recipe. What? You know how to make popcorn? Yeah, but do you know what to top it with?

To 4 cups popped popcorn add any of the following toppings:

1-2 Tablespoons soy margarine
¼ cup nutritional yeast
1 teaspoon garlic powder
1 teaspoon Spike

> *Per Cup: Calories: 93, Protein: 4 gm., Fat: 4 gm., Carbohydrates: 9 gm.*

1-2 Tablespoons soy margarine
¼ teaspoon cumin
1 teaspoon chili powder
½ teaspoon sea salt
¼ cup nutritional yeast

> *Per Cup: Calories: 93, Protein: 4 gm., Fat: 4 gm., Carbohydrates: 9 gm.*

1-2 Tablespoons soy margarine
¼ teaspoon coriander
¼ teaspoon sea salt
1 teaspoon curry powder
¼ cup nutritional yeast

> *Per Cup: Calories: 93, Protein: 4 gm., Fat: 4 gm., Carbohydrates: 9 gm.*

Herbed Onion Bread

Yield: 1 9" round
Prep: 15 minutes   Cook: 40 minutes

Easy, savory, starchy, filling. The perfect bread.

Dry ingredients:

1 cup whole wheat flour
1 cup corn meal flour
1 teaspoon baking powder
1 teaspoon sea salt
1 teaspoon tarragon
½ teaspoon oregano

Wet ingredients:

1 cup soymilk
⅔ cup water
1 Tablespoon olive
oil

1 cup fresh or frozen onions, chopped small

If using frozen onions, soak in hot water until tender. Use the soak liquid instead of the ⅔ cup water when mixing ingredients.

Preheat oven to 375°F. Combine dry ingredients in a bowl. In a separate bowl, whisk the wet ingredients together. Slowly add the wet to the dry, mixing thoroughly. Add the onions and pour mixture into a well oiled 9" skillet or 9" round cake pan and bake for 40 minutes.

Variation: Omit the herbs and onion and use 1 teaspoon each cinnamon and vanilla, 1 cup grated zucchini, a handful of raisins, and top with walnuts.

Per ⅛ Loaf: Calories: 137, Protein: 4 gm., Fat: 3 gm., Carbohydrates: 23 gm.

Simple Garlic Bread

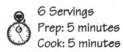

6 Servings
Prep: 5 minutes
Cook: 5 minutes

Forget all that slicing, melting, spreading, and wrapping. This is a simple recipe. Simply mahvelous.

1 loaf french, Cuban, or sourdough bread (unsliced)
6 cloves garlic, minced or 4 teaspoons pre-minced garlic
1 Tablespoon extra virgin olive oil
herb seasoning (Herbamare, Spike, Vegesal, etc. or one of the herb mixtures on page 22)

Split the loaf of bread lengthwise down the center, so you have a top and a bottom. Sprinkle the olive oil on both halves and spread evenly with a butter knife. Distribute the minced garlic evenly over the oiled bread and sprinkle herb seasoning over everything. Bake in 350°F oven or toaster oven until it begins to warm, about 10 minutes. Pop under the broiler for 30 seconds, slice, and serve warm.

Per Serving: Calories: 211, Protein: 8 gm., Fat: 5 gm., Carbohydrates: 33 gm.

Pita Toasts

2 Servings

A no-fat alternative for dunking in your favorite dip.

1 whole wheat pita round

Preheat oven to 350°F. Slice pita round in half, then quarters, then eighths. Separate the connecting end to come up with 16 pieces. Place on a cookie sheet in the preheated oven and bake until crisp, about 5 minutes.

Per Serving: Calories: 115, Protein: 5 gm., Fat: 0 gm., Carbohydrates: 25 gm.

DESSERTS

 Indicates recipes that take 15 minutes or less to *prepare and cook!*

Desserts have been a tough one. General grocery stores have failed to recognize anything but refined sugar as the sweetening agent in dessert products. Most pie shells and cookies contain lard and dairy products as ingredients. When sugar is mentioned first on the ingredients list, then you know the product is loaded with the drug ... uh, I mean, sweetener.

Desserts don't have to be self-indulgent junk, although that may be your particular kick in life. If you're going to the trouble of changing your diet, then the sweets in your life can be lifted to such heights that they're actually still bad for you, but not as damaging as using refined sugars. Yes indeed, you don't have to give up that special indulgence or the guilt that goes with it.

The sweeteners that you use in your concoctions are part of what can make or break the quality of your dessert. As if you care for quality–JUST MAKE IT SWEET! OK, we hear you, we hear you. The alternatives we are about to recommend to you are SWEET. Mind you, some are sweeter than others, but we'll point this out in the descriptions. Enough said, have a go!

Honey: Sweet enough to make your teeth scream for mercy or more. Those busy little bees will get you for stealing their honey. It can be used in baked goods, but the results have a cakey consistency when used in making cookies. Honey also adds a distinctive flavor all its own.

Maple Syrup: This sap, or blood, of a tree is very sweet and delicious. Use it for anything that needs sweetening, and don't forget to thank the trees for such a delightful contribution. Use half as much when substituting for refined sugar.

Rice Syrup: A mild grain sweetener made from brown rice. Good for diabetics because it is absorbed more slowly into the blood stream than white sugar, honey, or maple syrup. This gets sweeter to the taste the longer you don't eat refined sugar.

Barley Malt: Another mild sweetener made from the grain barley. Reminiscent of a light molasses flavor. Great in cookies.

Fructose: Concentrated fruit or corn sugar. Use half the amount or less when replacing refined white sugar in a recipe.

Date Sugar: Just what it says it is, in concentrated form. Use one for one in place of white sugar.

Blueberry Coffee Cake

Makes one 8" square cake- 9 servings (2 ⅔" x 2⅔")
Prep: 20 minutes   Bake: 30 minutes

Perhaps you're looking for a cake to take to a dinner and you're afraid the crowd won't appreciate anything other than Pillsbury. Well, here's the answer. Tried and tested on the Standard American Palate with outstanding results. Have no fear, this recipe will win you kudos at the next cooking event.

Dry ingredients:
  1 package Cake, Muffin, P an
  Bread Mix (see page 25) or:
    1 cup wheat or spelt flour
    1 cup rice flour
    2 teaspoons baking powder
    1 teaspoon baking soda
    1 teaspoon cinnamon
    ⅓ cup powdered fructose

Wet ingredients:
  2 cups soymilk
  4 Tablespoons corn oil
  1 teaspoon vanilla extract

1 cup blueberries, fresh or frozen

Topping:
  1 cup walnuts
  1 teaspoon cinnamon
  1 teaspoon powdered fructose
  1 Tablespoon corn oil

Preheat oven to 350°F. In a food processor puree the topping ingredients until finely chopped. Sprinkle the topping in the bottom of an oiled 8" square baking pan, and set aside. Combine dry ingredients in a bowl. Whisk together wet ingredients and add to the dry, mixing well. Stir in the blueberries at the end. Pour into the baking pan over the topping and bake for 30 minutes. Allow to cool, then invert the pan on a cake plate.

Per Serving: Calories: 326, Protein: 6 gm., Fat: 16 gm., Carbohydrates: 38 gm.

Almond Date Cake

Makes one 9" round bundt or 8" square pyrex pan
8 Servings
Prep: 15 minutes   Bake: 30 minutes

This is a nice dessert for a dinner party. Garnish with grapes and a fresh flower!

Dry ingredients:
1 package Cake, Muffin,
Pan Bread Mix #1
(page 25) or:
1 cup whole wheat or
spelt flour
1 cup rice or
unbleached flour
1 teaspoon baking soda
2 teaspoons baking powder
½ teaspoon sea salt
½ teaspoon cinnamon
½ cup dates, pitted, chopped

Wet ingredients:
1½ cups light amazake
or soymilk
2 Tablespoons corn oil
1 teaspoon vanilla extract
1 teaspoon almond extract
⅓ cup fructose

Glaze:
½ cup orange juice
2 Tablespoons barley malt or rice syrup
¼ teaspoon orange extract

Combine ingredients in a small saucepan. Heat only until the syrup melts, not to boiling. Place cake on a dessert plate, and spoon glaze over top.

Per Serving: Calories: 264, Protein: 5 gm., Fat: 5 gm., Carbohydrates: 50 gm.

Baked Apples

4 Servings
Prep: 10 minutes   Cook: 30 minutes

4 apples (McIntosh, Rome, or Cortland)
1 cup raisins
¼ cup walnuts, almonds, or pecans, chopped and
    roasted
2 Tablespoons peanut butter, tahini, or almond
    butter (optional)
¼ teaspoon cinnamon
pinch allspice (optional)
½ teaspoon vanilla extract
½ cup apple juice

Preheat oven to 375°F. Core and pierce apples with a fork in several places around the center to prevent bursting. Mix raisins, nuts, peanut butter, cinnamon, allspice, and vanilla in a small bowl. Fill center of each apple with raisin mixture. Place apples in a glass baking dish, and pour apple juice into pan. Cover with foil and bake for 30 minutes or until tender.

Per Apple: Calories: 251, Protein: 2 gm., Fat: 5 gm., Carbohydrates: 50 gm.

Almond Puff Bars

Makes eight 2" x 4" bars
Prep: 15 minutes   Chill: 30 minutes

Here's a fantastic way to use up those styrofoam-like rice cakes you stuck behind the soup cans or the puff cereal that is too plain to feed the kids. Yes, they're probably still good enough to use.

¼ cup almond butter
¼ cup barley malt
½ cup rice syrup
1 teaspoon almond extract
4 cups puffed grain cereal or crumbled rice cakes

OTHER OPTIONS:

¼ cup carob powder, carob chips, or raisins

In a small saucepan, over low heat, combine almond butter, barley malt, rice syrup, almond extract, and carob powder. When smooth and melted, combine with cereal and other optional ingredients in a medium size bowl. Mix well, making sure everything is coated with the mixture. Transfer to an 8" x 8" baking dish, cover, and chill for 30-60 minutes.

Per Bar: Calories: 143, Protein: 1 gm., Fat: 4 gm., Carbohydrates: 24 gm.

Low-Fat Brownies

Makes 8 2" x 4" bars
Prep: 15 minutes   Bake: 35 minutes

The key to this recipe is the rice flour. It bakes moist and chewy brownies that don't dry out like gluten based flours. No oil is used and leaving out the walnuts will lower the fat content even more. Top it with fruit-juice-sweetened jam or our Tofu Carob Frosting (see page 156) for an extra sweet taste treat.

Dry ingredients:
    1½ cups rice flour
    1 cup unroasted carob or cocoa powder
    ¼ teaspoon sea salt
    ⅔ cup chopped walnuts

Wet ingredients:
    1 (10 oz) package soft silken tofu
    1 teaspoon orange extract
    1 teaspoon vanilla extract
    ½ cup barley malt
    ½ cup maple syrup
    1 cup low-fat soymilk (plain, vanilla, or carob)

Preheat oven to 350°F. In a medium bowl, combine dry ingredients, except for walnuts. In a blender, puree the wet ingredients until smooth. Whisk together the wet and dry, and add the walnuts, mixing well. Pour into a lightly oiled 8" x 8" baking dish, and bake for 30 minutes.

Per Bar: Calories: 369, Protein: 7 gm., Fat: 8 gm., Carbohydrates: 68 gm.

Blueberry Cobbler

4 Servings
Prep: 5 minutes   Cook: 15 minutes

For a quick and delicious dessert, this one is a winner. You and your guests will have fun pointing out each other's blue teeth and lips so consider that before serving at a dinner party.

1 pint blueberries, peaches, or raspberries, fresh
    or frozen
⅛ - ¼ cup sweetener of choice
½ cup water
1 teaspoon arrowroot
2 large biscuits, halved
dash of cinnamon

Place fruit and sweetener in a small skillet and add ¼ cup water. Bring to a boil, reduce heat, and simmer for 6 minutes until tender. Dissolve the arrowroot in the remaining ¼ cup water, stir into the fruit mixture, and cook another 2 minutes, stirring frequently. Place the halved biscuits on top of the fruit compote, pressing them down into the liquid. Sprinkle with cinnamon and add a pat of soy margarine. Serve as is or with your favorite non-dairy frozen dessert. We found this one fun to eat without utensils! Just kidding!

Per Serving: Calories: 142, Protein: 1 gm., Fat: 3 gm., Carbohydrates: 28 gm.

Almond Oatmeal Flats

Yield: twelve 1 ½" cookies
Prep: 14 minutes   Bake: 20 minutes

These are the kind of sweets that we can confidently say:
"Bet you can't eat just one."

Dry Ingredients:
Use one bag of pre-mixed Cookie, Crisp, Crust
mixture #3 (see page 25)
or:
½ cup whole wheat flour
½ cup ground almonds
1½ cups coarsely ground oatmeal
⅛ teaspoon sea salt
1 teaspoon cinnamon

Wet Ingredients:
⅓ cup vegetable oil
1 cup rice syrup or   ½ cup honey or maple syrup
½ teaspoon almond extract
1 teaspoon vanilla extract

Preheat oven to 350°F. Mix dry ingredients well. Mix wet ingredients and add to dry. Make individual cookies and place on lightly oiled cookie sheets, or pat into a lightly oiled 9" x 13" pan. Bake for 20 minutes.

These are not meant to be real sweet, but if you want that extra sugar rush, then spread some fruit sweetened raspberry jam on them while still hot from the oven. "And paradise is here now."

Each Cookie: Calories: 189, Protein: 4 gm., Fat: 10 gm.,
Carbohydrates: 22 gm.

Crisp Topping

Yield: 2 cups of rumbles
Prep: 5 minutes   Bake: 20 minutes

Invented for a late night sweet tooth. The title came later.

1½ cups quick-cooking or rolled oats
¼ cup whole wheat flour (pastry is best) or
    rice flour
1 Tablespoon corn oil
½ teaspoon cinnamon
⅓ cup maple syrup, brown rice syrup, or honey
2 Tablespoons almonds, chopped (optional)
1 teaspoon almond extract
pinch of sea salt

Preheat oven to 350°F. Combine everything in a bowl, and mix well. Spread out loosely on a cookie sheet, and bake for 20 minutes. Allow to cool, break apart into crumbles, and put on top of ice cream, fruit compote, etc.

Per ¼ Cup: Calories: 131, Protein: 3 gm., Fat: 3 gm.,
Carbohydrates: 23 gm.

Peanut Butter Chews

Yield: eight 2" x 4" bars
Prep: 10 minutes   Bake: 15 minutes

This page has been specially treated to withstand grease stains from the peanut butter. We're that sure you're going to make these again and again.

½ cup peanut butter
½ cup maple syrup, honey or rice syrup
1 cup oats, quick-cooking or rolled
1 teaspoon vanilla

Preheat oven to 350°F. Mix all ingredients using a sturdy wooden spoon. Batter will be thick. Press evenly into a lightly oiled 8" x 8" square pyrex pan. Spread your favorite jam across the top, and bake for 15 minutes.

Each Bar: Calories: 201, Protein: 5 gm., Fat: 8 gm., Carbohydrates: 26 gm.

Smoothies

Prep: 5 minutes

Now these are the breakfasts we dream about on those hot summer mornings. Cold, fruity, thick, and creamy shakes without the skyrocketing calories from cream, ice cream, chocolate, and sugary, syrupy fruit. There is one catch, though. You need to freeze a batch of ripe bananas in order to get the thick, creamy consistency. In fact, go ahead and freeze any ripe fruit, and create your own taste sensations! Start your blenders, please ...

Your Basic Fruit Smoothie

Yield: one 16 ounce glass

1 cup apple juice (unsweetened, please)
1 peeled, frozen banana
½ cup frozen fruit of choice (strawberries,
    blueberries, peaches, melon, etc.)

Pour apple juice into blender. Chunk up banana in 2" pieces and toss into juice. Wipe up apple juice from counter. Place lid on blender and buzz until creamy. Add second fruit of choice and buzz again. This should produce a thick shake, but if you like it thicker, go ahead and add more fruit.

Per Glass: Calories: 247, Protein: 1 gm., Fat: 0 gm., Carbohydrates: 58 gm.

The Return Of Your Basic Fruit Smoothie

1 cup pineapple juice
1 peeled, frozen banana
½ cup frozen strawberries
2 dates, pitted please

Buzzzzzzzzzzzzzzzzzzzzzzzzzzzzzzzzzzzzzzzzzzzzzzzzzzzzzzzzzzzz. Ahhhhh!

Calories: 309, Protein: 3 gm., Fat: 0 gm., Carbohydrates: 73 gm.

Your Basic Fruit Smoothie Lives Again

½ cup coconut milk
½ cup pineapple juice
1 peeled, frozen banana
1 cup frozen pineapple
2 dates, see above

Buzzzzzzzzzzzzzzzzzzzzzzzzzzzzzzzzzzzzzzzzzzzzzzzzzzzzzzzzz. Ya Maahn!

Calories: 427, Protein: 3 gm., Fat: 21 gm., Carbohydrates: 48 gm.

Indulgent Shake And Jiggle

 One 16 oz serving
Prep: 6 minutes

We won't lie to you, this is called indulgent because it is delicious and loaded with calories. For a lighter version try it without the banana, the nuts, or the guilt.

1 cup low-fat vanilla soymilk
1 cup low-fat soy ice cream of your choice
1 medium banana (fresh or frozen)
dash of vanilla
1 Tablespoon vanilla protein powder (optional)
¼ cup nuts of choice (optional)

Blend and then freeze for 15 minutes.

Per Serving: Calories: 504, Protein: 9 gm., Fat: 20 gm., Carbohydrates: 72 gm.

Banana Pudding

 Yield: 2 cups
Prep: 5 minutes

This is how to fall in love with the versatility of tofu.

1 (10 oz) package soft silken tofu, refrigerated
2 ripe bananas
1 teaspoon vanilla extract or ¼ teaspoon almond
    extract
¼ cup maple syrup or to taste

Blend all together in a blender or food processor until smooth. That's all.

Per Cup: Calories: 313, Protein: 11 gm., Fat: 6 gm., Carbohydrates: 52 gm.

Tootsie Rolls II, Revenge Of The Sweet Tooth

Yield: 24 finger size rolls
Prep: 8 minutes   Chill: 2 hours

Very yummy. Very, very yummy. Requires hands on.

1 cup carob powder
⅓ cup peanut butter
⅓ cup maple syrup, honey, or rice syrup
½ cup wheat germ

With a strong spoon mix all ingredients together well. Then dig in with your hands to complete the mixing. Mold into tootsie roll shape, and freeze until firm, about 2 hours (if you can wait).

Each Roll: Calories: 61, Protein: 2 gm., Fat: 2 gm., Carbohydrates: 10 gm.

Fudge II

Makes sixteen 1½" squares
Prep: 15 minutes   Chill: 30 minutes

Oh happy days! Valentines, Christmas, Easter, Hanukkah, Monday,
Tuesday, Wednesday ...

¼ cup maple syrup or honey
2 Tablespoons safflower or canola oil
1½ Tablespoons cocoa or carob powder
¼ cup almond or peanut butter

½ teaspoon vanilla extract
1 cup rolled oats
¼ cup soymilk powder
½ cup chopped walnuts and/or coconut

Place first 4 ingredients in a small saucepan and bring to a boil. Cook and stir for less than 1 minute. Remove from heat and stir in remaining ingredients. This will be very thick, but persevere in mixing these ingredients together. If too dry, add 1 Tablespoon hot water. Pat down into a ½" thick rectangle in a glass baking dish or cookie sheet, and chill for ½ hour. Slice and serve.

Each Piece: Calories: 68, Protein: 2 gm., Fat: 5 gm., Carbohydrates: 6 gm.

Chocolate Almond Pudding

4 Servings (⅓ cup each)
Prep: 5 minutes (assuming you have a batch of almonds already roasted. I mean, who doesn't?)
Chill: 30 minutes

The easiest, the best.

1 (10 oz) package silken tofu
⅓ cup cocoa or carob powder
¼-⅓ cup maple syrup or honey (How sweet do you like it?)
1 Tablespoon smooth almond butter
1 teaspoon almond extract
1 teaspoon orange extract
2 Tablespoons roasted almonds, chopped (as garnish)

Place all ingredients except the almonds in a blender or food processor. Puree until smooth and creamy. Chill in individual custard cups and top with a sprinkling of roasted almonds.

Per Serving: Calories: 218, Protein: 8 gm., Fat: 9 gm., Carbohydrates: 26 gm.

Tofu Whipped ... Cream

Yield: 1 cup
Prep: 5 minutes   Chill: 30 minutes

A thicker version of whipped cream. Serve as a topping for fruit and desserts.

1 (10 oz) package silken tofu
¼ cup maple syrup, rice syrup, or honey
1 teaspoon vanilla

Buzzzzzzzzzzzzzzzzzzzzzzzzzzzzzzzzzzzzzzzzzzzzzzzzzzzzzzzzzzzzzzz until very smooth. Chill.

Per 2 Tablespoons: Calories: 59, Protein: 2 gm., Fat: 1 gm., Carbohydrates: 9 gm.

Tofu Carob Frosting

 Yield: 2 ½ cups
Prep: 5 minutes

1 (10 oz) package firm silken tofu
⅔ cup carob or cocoa powder
¼ cup honey or maple syrup
½ teaspoon vanilla
¼ cup almond butter

Buzzzzzzzzzzzzzzzzzzzzzzzzzzzzzzzzzzzzzzzzzzzzzzzzzzzzzzzzzzzzz until smooth. Spread on your favorite cake, cookie, or the palm of your hand, and chill.

Per Tablespoon: Calories: 28, Protein: 1 gm., Fat: 1 gm., Carbohydrates: 3 gm.

Index

Ask your store to carry these books, or you may order directly from:

The Book Publishing Company
P.O. Box 99
Summertown, TN 38483

Or call: 1-800-695-2241
*Please add $2.50 per book
for shipping*

Almost-No Fat Cookbook 10.95
American Harvest 11.95
Burgers 'n Fries 'n Cinnamon Buns 6.95
Cooking with Gluten and Seitan 7.95
Ecological Cooking: Recipes to Save the Planet 10.95
Fabulous Beans 9.95
From A Traditional Greek Kitchen 9.95
Good Time Eatin' in Cajun Country 9.95
Holiday Diet Book 9.95
Indian Vegetarian Cooking at Your House 12.95
Instead of Chicken, Instead of Turkey 9.95
Kids Can Cook 9.95
New Farm Vegetarian Cookbook 8.95
Now & Zen Epicure 17.95
Olive Oil Cookery 11.95
Peaceful Cook 8.95
Physician's Slimming Guide, Neal D. Barnard, M.D. 5.95
  Also by Dr. Barnard:
  Foods That Cause You To Lose Weight 12.95
  The Power of Your Plate (Revised) 12.95
Shiitake Way $7.95
Shoshoni Cookbook 12.95
Simply Heavenly 19.95
Soups For All Seasons 9.95
The Sprout Garden 8.95
Starting Over: Learning to Cook with Natural Foods 10.95
Tempeh Cookbook 10.95
Ten Talents (Vegetarian Cookbook) 18.95
Tofu Cookery 14.95
Tofu Quick & Easy 7.95
TVP® Cookbook 6.95
Uncheese Cookbook 11.95
Uprisings: The Whole Grain Bakers' Book 13.95
Vegetarian Cooking for People with Diabetes 10.95